THE AUTHOR ESTATE HANDBOOK

HOW TO ORGANIZE YOUR AFFAIRS AND LEAVE A LEGACY (LARGE PRINT EDITION)

M.L. RONN

Special thank you to the following people on Patreon who supported this book: BB Dee, Matty Dalrymple, Cariad Eccleston, Stephen Frans, Michael Guishard, Jon Howard, Beth Jackson, Megan Mong, S. Chipasula Perry, Lynda Washington, and Etta Welk.

For more helpful writing tips and advice, subscribe to the Author Level Up YouTube channel: www. youtube.com/authorlevelup.

and/province. It is highly recommended that you use this book as a starting point and that you ultimately seek the counsel of a skilled lawyer, financial advisor, and accountant to build an estate plan that works for you and your family.

CONTENTS

ORGANIZING YOUR ESTATE

THE SILVER BULLETS OF DOOM

OTHER ESTATE ORGANIZATION ITEMS

INTRODUCTION

Dear Author,

I hate to tell you this, but you have just died. You are now a ghost, hovering around to see what has happened after your passing.

After the ink on your obituary dries, after the funeral is over and your family has gone home to grieve, after your casket is set in the ground or your urn is placed on a shelf, and after the initial flurry of respects and condolences from your friends quiets down to nothing, the world will keep on spinning as if you never existed.

Your loved ones will grieve, but even they too will move on. Your only marks on the world will be the memories your friends and loved ones had of you, how you made them feel, and (the reason you're reading this) your books.

In your twilight solitude as a ghost, you have a lot of time now to reflect on the literary estate you left behind.

What will you see?

If you're reading this, I think you already know the answer.

You probably picked up this book because you have no idea where to start in planning your author estate. The concept of wills, powers of attorney, advance medical directives, and all the other classic estate planning advice are overwhelming enough, but the **author** part—that makes it unbearable.

If you don't take care of the **author** part of your estate planning, then you're guaranteeing that your books will die with you.

This book will help you start the process of planning for what will happen to your books after you die. It will give you a fighting chance at ensuring that your books outlive you.

To read this book means to face your mortality, and that's not easy. This is a sensitive subject that may be difficult for you. However, it's painfully necessary. Death is a fact of life, and the sooner you face it, the sooner you will create the author legacy you want.

When you finish this book, you'll have what you need to take the first steps with clarity and confidence.

MY ESTATE PLANNING STORY

Many people take a sudden interest in estate planning after witnessing someone die and leave a mess, such as a parent dying without a will.

My story is the opposite.

In June 2021, I lost a grandfather to old age. He was part of the Greatest Generation, and he grew up in the Great Depression. He was extremely frugal and paid cash for everything. He kept an old school ledger and balanced his checkbook weekly. He never used a computer in his life and never had an email account.

Before he passed away, he stressed that he didn't want to be a burden on the family. When he passed, he was true to his word.

He had a will that clearly outlined his wishes (which my family knew well before he died). His estate was settled in just a few months with no squabbles among his children. There were no lawsuits or other nightmarish stories you often hear about estates.

Losing him was tough on the family, but we found peace much faster because his affairs were so well taken care of.

When I think of my grandfather, I remember the time we spent together and how he set such a positive example, but mostly, I remember how kind he was to be so organized.

He didn't have to be so organized, but he was. So many people take an "I'm dead, so who cares?" approach to their estate planning (or lack thereof), and it causes so much pain for their loved ones. My grandfather's approach was, "I'm going to be dead, so I need to make sure it is taken care of."

My grandfather didn't draw up his estate plan overnight; it was the result of many decisions he made early and often.

To this day, I'm still in awe of how he did it. My grandfather taught me an important lesson in organization, but most importantly, he taught me how to die. I know it sounds morbid, but I want to die like he did.

When you think about life in the twenty-first century, dying like my grandfather did is a phenomenal challenge. So much of our lives are online, digital, and difficult to corral. It's so much more complex and dynamic due to the Internet and the breakneck pace of technology.

Being an author makes estate planning even harder. In my case, I have over 70 books (and counting), a

YouTube channel with over 300 videos, four websites, and many, many other miscellaneous copyrights. At the time of this writing, I control over 1,500 copyrights. I also have a significant digital footprint, with hundreds of accounts that I've created with different companies over the years.

I set out to learn how I could create an estate that looked after my family the same way my grandfather did—adjusted for the frenetic twenty-first century, and, you know, all the author stuff.

I decided that it was time to start my author estate planning journey, so I did what most writers do when they want to learn something—I wrote a book about it.

A LITTLE MORE ABOUT ME

I have a unique background.

I went to law school (but I'm not an attorney). My legal education is limited and I am not licensed to practice law, but I do have a legal background.

I am also an insurance executive at a global insurance company. I have built a career helping individuals and businesses plan for the future and deal with unexpected disasters, and I have been quite successful at it.

These skills combined with my experience as a prolific author give me a different angle on this topic that I hope will make this book more useful to you.

WHO THIS BOOK IS FOR

This book is for authors who want to plan their estates. It's primarily for independent (self-published) authors and authorpreneurs, but traditionally-published authors can benefit from this book as well.

This book may also be helpful for the people that authors designate as their executors and heirs, but only if the author is still alive. This book can help authors and their heirs set expectations and get on the same page. The content in this book is a good conversation starter with your estate attorney.

DISCLAIMERS

This book is full of advice, but none of it is legal, financial, or tax advice. No matter what I say (and how strongly I say it), it is just a suggestion.

If there's one thing I learned on my estate planning journey, it's just how few resources there are for authors. The estate of an author is radically different from that of a regular person, yet if you search for the topic on the Internet, you won't find very much. I believe this is because estate planning is lawyer territory, and that scares a lot of people.

But, there are a lot of important elements that are unique to authors that your lawyer may not ask you about. My goal is to merely bring up many of the issues I encountered in my own journey so you're aware of them. As with any problem, awareness is half the battle. Estate planning is an unbelievably complex topic with many, many layers.

It is up to you to determine the best way to plan your estate. You cannot plan an estate without the help of a skilled attorney, accountant, and financial adviser, period. Use this book as a starting point to seek specific help in your country, state, or province. Don't use it as a substitute for legal advice.

And speaking of countries, I've tried to make this book as international as possible. Though I am an American, I've been careful to keep the topic at a high level so that it applies to as many non-Americans as possible. I used Australia, Canada, the United Kingdom, and the United States as the basis for my research. I can't promise that this book will be one hundred percent accurate for your country, but I at least tried to keep non-Americans in mind as I wrote it.

Again, use this book as a starting point, not as a substitute for legal advice.

IMPORTANT RULES OF THUMB

Estate planning is not one-size-fits-all. Everyone's goals and visions of how they want their author estate to be handled will be different. Season the advice in this book to taste. My goal is simply to get you thinking about this so that you can clarify your own goals and take the first steps.

It's never too early to start estate planning. I don't care if you're in your twenties and healthy. You're still living on borrowed time. Untimely deaths are especially tragic when you're young. Young people never think they're going to die unexpectedly, and they leave behind colossal messes as a result, especially if they have young families.

It's never too late to start estate planning. The good news is that if you're alive, you can rectify past mistakes and start now.

Something is better than nothing. If you already have a will, that's great, but it's only the first step. If you've already taken some of the other steps in this book, that's wonderful, and I commend you. This book will help you take even more steps. That said…

You'll never be able to plan for everything. Estate planning is a gigantic topic with many parts, and each part has layers. Your heirs will almost certainly run into some kind of problem after you're gone no matter how well you plan. All you can do is the best you can to eliminate the most obvious stumbling blocks for your heirs.

Simplicity is best for heirs. Running a writing business is complex. You know exactly what needs to be done to publish and sell a book. Your heirs probably do not. Remember that they're going to be grieving immediately after your death; anything you can do to make things easy for them will be much appreciated. If your heirs are publishing-savvy, more power to them, but I predict that most are not.

Longer term, also remember that your heirs have interests and passions of their own, and, honestly, asking them to inherit a writing business is a tremendous responsibility that they may not entirely understand until you're gone. They may eventually come to see it as a burden. You must think of ways to simplify the management of your estate so that it is not too burdensome for your heirs.

The best practices for running an author business almost always result in increased complexity for your heirs, which works against the previous rule. I can guarantee you that your writing business today is probably not simple. In fact, you are almost certainly doing the opposite of making things simple because the profession requires it. Let me give you some examples:

- The proper way to run an international writing business is to "go wide," meaning that you sell your book anywhere and everywhere you can. This requires you to open many accounts with many retailers, all of whom have different dashboards, guidelines, and payment terms. Imagine how disorienting that will be for your heirs when they have to log in to not one, not two, but many dashboards just to figure out what is going on.
- At the time of this writing, pay-per-click (PPC) advertising is a commonly-accepted marketing technique. However, you might spend $100 which boosts your sales, but

you might make only $20 in profit. If you stop advertising, your sales will virtually disappear. Put another way, you're paying for sales. Mastering PPC is an exercise in patience and practice, something that will be foreign and overwhelming for your heirs if they have never done it before.

- More successful authors can afford to outsource work by hiring virtual assistants (VAs) or even hiring employees. VAs may handle tasks such as emails, marketing, and website maintenance, among many other things. Hiring a VA frees up the author to do other more important tasks. Upon an author's death, many tasks that the VA did for them will probably no longer be needed, but for those that are, your heirs may not know how to do those tasks because they were historically outsourced. If the author leaves no documentation, it can cause massive confusion.

Don't misunderstand me. I'm not saying that you should go exclusive to Amazon, stop PPC advertising, or never hire VAs so you can make things simple. I am saying that you need to recognize the contradiction.

Your heirs will need simplicity, but that often runs contrary to running a profitable writing business while you're alive. If you can hold these two competing interests in your mind as you plan for your estate, you'll increase the chances of solving the problem gracefully.

Plan at your own pace, but do plan. As I said, this is a big topic, and you won't be able to solve it overnight. Take a few steps at a time. But you must take steps. Remember, no one is promised tomorrow.

If you're ready to join me on this wild journey of estate planning, turn the page and let's get into it.

—M.L. Ronn
Des Moines, Iowa
December 24, 2021

THE THREE STAGES OF ESTATE MANAGEMENT

First, let's define "estate." According to the Oxford Dictionary, it is "all the money and property owned by a particular person, especially at death."

Your estate does not exist until you die—thus why you must plan for its eventual existence. Such a plan is called an estate plan. In an estate plan, you must plan for how your money and property (also known as "assets") will be distributed. The part of an author's estate that contains the copyrights is sometimes called a literary estate.

Your "executor" (also "executrix" or "personal representative") is the person you designate to run your estate, settle your affairs, and handle the money, usually designated in your will. A court must appoint your executor. If you don't designate someone, a court will do it for you.

Your "heirs" (also known as "beneficiaries") are the people you designate to receive (or benefit from) your assets. They are usually spouses, children, or grandchildren, but not always.

(Moving forward, I use the term "heirs" to encompass both your executor(s) and heirs to keep things simpler. Just recognize that they are not always the same, but they can be. An executor is usually an heir, but an heir is not always an executor.)

When most people die, their assets are distributed, their estates are settled, and everyone moves on.

As an author, you have created an estate where your heirs don't have that luxury, at least if you want them to continue earning money from your books. The traditional parts of your estate will be settled like everyone else's, but the **author** part of your estate will be an ongoing responsibility.

In the case of your books, you must plan for how they will be managed. First, you have to get your affairs in order and become extremely organized. Next, you must make sure you select the right person to assume the responsibilities of being your executor.

You must also think about how your heirs will keep your books discoverable, available for sale, and keep the money flowing. You must also plan for future opportunities that may come to your heirs as well, as it's not uncommon for licensing deals to happen after an author is dead, especially if one of their books takes on a new life. If Hollywood wanted to turn one of your books into a movie after your death, how would they contact your heirs?

THE THREE STAGES OF ESTATE MANAGEMENT

It's helpful to think of your estate planning in three stages.

First, there is the **Planning** stage. During this stage, you must figure out what your goals are, and you must accomplish the fundamentals: a will, power of attorney, and advance directive, to name a few. This is also when you decide on things like trusts and life insurance. There are many choices, but a skilled estate attorney, financial adviser, and accountant can help.

Second, once you've addressed the fundamentals, there is the **Organization** stage. In the case of your books, a will only outlines how your copyrights will be distributed (if it mentions them, and it should), but it doesn't say anything about how to manage them. A will won't tell your heirs which bank accounts your book sales go to or where your book files are if changes need to be made. A will especially won't disclose your passwords.

The Organization stage is all about getting organized so that you don't leave a mess. I consider this to be the most difficult and overwhelming part of estate planning.

And finally, there is the **Management** stage. This is unique to authors and creatives, and it begins when you die. During this stage, your heirs begin managing your estate per your wishes. This is when all successes and mistakes will become clear. If you executed the Planning and Organization stages thoughtfully, your heirs will thank you. If you screwed up, they may very well hate you. I don't use the word hate lightly—after we discuss some of the horror stories that can happen if you don't plan properly, I think you'll agree that your heirs will be entitled to some strong feelings.

Every author estate will be managed differently. Some heirs will be more hands-on than others. You can think of an estate as being managed in one of three levels:

- Level 1: Maintenance. The heirs keep your books available for sale, discoverable for readers, and they make sure that income is received. This is the bare minimum amount of work that needs to be done.
- Level 2: Active. The heirs do everything in Level 1 plus refresh and renew your titles from time to time. This requires more work and an understanding of the business.

Your heirs can do the work themselves or outsource it to professionals who can help.

- Level 3: Aggressive. The heirs do everything in Levels 1 and 2 plus seek to grow the estate. This could mean releasing posthumous titles, pursuing licensing deals, making your books into movies, and so on. This requires the most amount of work, and this is the rarest type of author estate.

Think about your heirs and consider at which level they would manage your estate. Most authors are probably operating at Level 3, but it's not reasonable to expect our heirs to put the same level of energy into the business that we do. Adjust your plan accordingly based on your heirs' desires and capabilities.

The Management stage is outside the scope of this book.

As you progress through this book, keep the three stages of estate management in mind.

PLANNING YOUR ESTATE

YOUR LAST WILL AND TESTAMENT

A will is a written legal document that outlines how your property and money will be distributed after your death.

A will names an executor who will manage your estate.

By law, you're not required to have a will, but you should strongly consider it. Wills prevent common scenarios that can cause problems after you die, such as who gets what, what happens if you die simultaneously with your spouse, and the legal guardianship of minor children, just to name a few.

. . .

LET'S TALK ABOUT PROBATE

Let's talk about probate because the term is often used when discussing wills, and it carries a lot of negative baggage.

Probate is the validation of a will by a court. It is also the court-supervised division of a person's assets. Probate exists to close estates in an orderly manner and protect creditors.

When you die, for legal purposes, you will die one of two ways: with a will (called dying "testate") or without a will (dying "intestate").

If you die without a will, a court determines how your assets will be distributed depending on the laws in your state, province, or territory. We can both agree that letting a court decide the terms of your estate is a terrible idea.

With a valid will, you get to choose how your property is divided. That is one of the most important reasons to make a will.

Many people seek to avoid probate entirely because they understandably don't want the state involved in their affairs. That may not be entirely possible. For example, if you have minor children, probate is unavoidable because guardians will have to be appointed by the court.

Probate gets a bad name, but with proper planning and a will that clearly outlines your wishes, a skilled attorney can get you through the proceedings much faster. In the case of my grandfather, his estate was settled in less than six months, which was blazing fast.

When you die, your attorney will deliver your will to the probate court, which will open proceedings. Your estate will be created and it will be time to apportion your assets.

The court will appoint your executor and give them the legal power to manage your estate. The executor will inventory all your real estate, personal property, copyrights, and other unique property you own. They will prepare what is called a reporting inventory (or simply, "inventory"). The reporting inventory is used to determine how much property you have and to value the estate for tax purposes. The executor will also work with your estate attorney, pay debts, sell your property, and take any other actions requested in your will and/or required by the state. Once the executor fulfills all obligations, the court will allow them to close the estate.

Some property types generally do not pass through probate: any property left to a surviving spouse, money in bank accounts with certain joint ownership or payable-on-death (POD) designations, retirement accounts, life insurance, and property held in a living trust, to name a few. You'll need to see what types of property are exempt from probate in your country, state, province, or territory.

Property that doesn't go through probate reduces the size of your taxable estate, similar to how tax deductions reduce the size of your taxable income. Depending on where you live, if you manage your estate following probate property exemption laws, you can maximize the amount of property that stays out of probate and maintain some privacy and flexibility for your heirs. This will also help you reduce your probate costs.

That said, you'll still have to pay your executor and your attorney fees as required by your local laws. Probate is a lot of work.

Probate can also be long. I made it sound simple, but the reality is that it is anything but. People who go through probate often are overwhelmed and frustrated with the lack of control they have, especially if the deceased did not plan properly. Even though you may not be able to avoid probate entirely, it's a smart idea to strategize with your estate attorney about how you can reduce your probate costs.

NOW, LET'S TALK ABOUT WILLS

Should you have a will? It depends on your situation, but you probably should. If you don't, you will definitely want an attorney's advice—

dying intestate without proper planning can be a costly mistake. Probate can be very expensive.

I can't tell you what should be in your will, other than that it should be drafted by a licensed attorney who specializes in wills and trusts in your area.

Wills are not cheap to create, but the money you'll spend on the will is a pittance compared to the money your heirs will have to spend in probate court.

There are online services and do-it-yourself-will software, but I strongly discourage you from using them. They're not designed for authors, and the chances are too high that you will make a mistake or that the will won't cover everything it should. No matter what country you live in, estate law is complex.

I always recommend a licensed, skilled attorney when making a will. DIY wills might be fine for regular people, but you own copyrights, which means you're not a regular person.

.   .   .

AN AUTHOR WHO DIED WITHOUT A WILL: STIEG LARSSON

Stieg Larsson was a prominent Swedish journalist and author of the **Millennium** crime series. He died suddenly of a heart attack in 2004. His books, published posthumously, were hits, and in death, he is still one of the most successful bestselling authors in the world.

What you may not know about Larsson is that he died without a will. Larsson's story is a cautionary tale of what can happen if you don't make a will.

As a journalist, Larsson wrote pieces that railed against the Far Right in his country, a position that placed him in constant danger.

Larsson lived with his longtime partner, but they did not marry because Swedish law dictated that married couples had to disclose their address to the public. Doing so could have endangered Larsson's life.

After Larsson's death, it was discovered that he did not leave a valid will. His family found a 1977 will that left all his work to the Swedish Socialist Party, but it was determined to be invalid because it was not signed in the presence of witnesses (another good example of why you should always hire an attorney). As a result, Larsson's copyrights went to his father and brother rather than his partner. Larsson reportedly did not have a good relationship with his father. He may not have even known that he had a brother.

Since Larsson was not married, his partner had no rights to his property, even though passing the copyrights to her may have been what he would have wanted.

What **would** he have wanted? Since he didn't leave a will, we'll never know.

There have been claims that Larsson's father and brother have done things with the copyrights that Larsson would never have approved of, and that run contrary to the spirit of his work. His father, brother, and partner have been in a bitter feud since his death.

Despite the massive cash flow his books created, Larsson's legacy isn't what it could have been.

Larsson could have prevented all of this by drafting a will that left his estate and copyrights to his partner.

However, just having a will is not enough.

AN AUTHOR WHO DIED WITHOUT A PROPERLY DRAFTED WILL: MICHAEL CRICHTON

At the time of his death in 2008, Michael Crichton was one of the bestselling authors in the world (and still is). His works such as **Jurassic Park** and **Westworld** were intensely popular and still endure today.

Crichton was married five times. When he died from cancer, his fifth wife was pregnant with his unborn child.

Crichton had a will, but he never got around to updating it. Because of that, he disinherited his unborn child because he didn't update his will before the baby was born. The will had a provision that disinherited anyone making a claim who was not listed in the will.

A bitter legal battle ensued between Crichton's 20-year-old daughter and his fifth wife. His wife filed a lawsuit to have the court grant part of Crichton's estate to his son under a loophole in California law. She was ultimately successful, but it cost a lot of money and stress that would have been avoided if Crichton had simply updated his will in the first place.

Crichton's story illustrates that having a will is not enough. It needs to reflect your wishes correctly and it needs to be current.

If Stieg Larsson's and Michael Crichton's stories scare you, there's good news. If you don't have a will, you can start one today by calling an estate attorney for a consultation. If you have a will but it's not up-to-date, call your attorney. You can probably get your will updated within a week.

However, it's not enough to keep your will current. There's another pitfall to discuss.

COPYRIGHTS IN YOUR WILL

As it pertains to your personal affairs, a skilled attorney will help you avoid most major pitfalls in drafting your will. Problems such as guardianship of minor children and the division of your assets can easily be addressed.

However, you should be careful because there's one area in an author's will where even a skilled attorney can make a mistake: copyrights. Unless you tell the attorney you're an author, they may not ask if you own copyrights. And even if you tell them, they may not understand copyright law.

Copyrights are intellectual property, which is a specialized and complicated area of the law, but they are still considered property like everything else you own. As we discussed, a will outlines how your property is distributed after your death. If you don't describe how you want your **copyrights** to be distributed, then there could be unfortunate consequences.

Let me tell you a cautionary tale about my first will. I had it made just after I became a father. I was in my mid-twenties and I wanted to make sure that my wife and I provided for my daughter if something were to happen to us.

At the time, I was getting my writing career off the ground and had only published a few books. I didn't know very much about copyright (or wills) at the time.

I had the foresight to tell my attorney that I was an author and that I wanted my copyrights addressed in the will.

Here's what one article in the will said: "If my spouse survives me, I give her all my clothing, jewelry, automobiles, household furniture and furnishings, recreational equipment, **copyrights**, and all personal effects used by me about my person or home."

Looking back on it, it was smart to include copyrights in my will. I don't know if this was the proper way to word my wishes, but I give the attorney some credit.

But the next clause would have completely wrecked my estate: "If my spouse does not survive me, I direct my executor to give my copyrights and any income in the form of copyrights to my children in equal shares. If my child is still a minor, the income from the copyrights shall be held by the Trust created in Article X and the decisions regarding the copyrights will be made by their guardian."

Let's break the language down so you can see how the attorney screwed me.

- The will creates a trust that holds my copyright income (called a "testamentary trust"). A testamentary trust is a trust that is created by a will. It increases the costs of probate and it also ensures that my copyrights will be public and part of my taxable estate. What if, due to a twist in fate, I became hugely successful, with millions in book sales, movie deals, and more? All of that would have been subject to estate taxes upon my death, and the taxes could have been substantial. That's a tragedy because there is a legal way to avoid this!

- Coupling guardianship and literary executorship was a bad idea for my situation at the time. I gave the decision-making power of the copyrights to my mother, who also received guardianship of my daughter if my wife and I both died. That's a lot for one person to handle. If my mom didn't survive me, my mother-in-law would receive guardianship and the copyrights. My mother-in-law doesn't speak English and is not Internet-savvy—and she would possess all my copyrights. I love my mother-in-law, and I know she would raise my daughter well, but she's not the right person to manage my **copyrights**. My attorney knew all of this, but they never pointed it out because they didn't understand the nature of copyright.

There are other legal problems with the language, but I share this so you can learn from my mistakes. When I created this will, I was a new dad, working a stressful job, and I was extremely sleep-deprived due to taking care of a newborn. I read the will, but I didn't really understand it and the potential consequences. My attorney didn't understand the nature of my copyrights either.

I did not hire the right attorney. The attorney did a decent job with the personal aspects of the will, but they had no clue about copyright. The average, everyday client doesn't own copyrights, so my attorney probably wasn't used to seeing them. And of course, because I didn't know any better, I took my attorney's word on everything, which could have been an estate-ending mistake.

Upon discovering that language in my will, I immediately contacted a new estate attorney to start a new will from scratch that properly addressed my copyrights. At the same time, I consulted with a licensed copyright lawyer in my state to get his counsel on the best way to craft language that would achieve my wishes. The copyright lawyer works with authors, creatives, and brands, but he doesn't do wills or trusts. Therefore, when the estate attorney sent me a draft of the will, I discussed it with my copyright attorney, who provided feedback and tweaks to the copyright-related wording. This way, the estate attorney handled the personal aspects of the will with great skill and care, and he supplemented any gaps in his knowledge with my copyright attorney's expertise.

And this time around, you can bet that I went through their work with a scrutinizing eye!

When we finished the new will, I burned the old one in my fireplace and took a big sigh of relief.

WHAT HAPPENS WHEN YOU DO NOT INCLUDE COPYRIGHTS IN YOUR WILL

What happens when you don't include your copyrights in your will?

Going back to my original will, let me share another article with you. It is commonly called the "residuary clause," and it addresses any assets not covered explicitly by the will. It functions like a safety net in case the deceased forgets about something or acquires new property after executing the will.

Here's how it reads: "If my spouse survives me, I give her the residue of my estate."

This means that my spouse gets all property not explicitly mentioned in the previous article I cited.

Next, the article addresses what happens if my spouse does not survive me: "If my spouse does not survive, I give the residue of my estate to the XXX Trust. The trust should be distributed one-fourth to my mother, one-fourth to my mother-in-law, with the rest to be held in trust for my daughter."

Since my original will mentioned my copyrights, the residuary clause didn't apply to them.

But let's pretend that I did not explicitly mention copyrights in my will. If so, then the residuary clause would apply to them.

Put another way, per the will's residuary clause, if my spouse did not survive me, my copyrights would have been placed in a testamentary trust created by the will, with half of my copyrights split between my mother and mother-in-law, and the remainder going to my daughter.

But what does that mean, actually? Which copyrights would my mother get? My mother-in-law? Which books? Which formats? Would my mother get the e-book versions but my mother-in-law would get the trade paperbacks? Remember, a copyright is not a single right—it's a bundle of infinite rights. You can't divide it up like that without disastrous results.

I don't know what your residuary clause says other than that it will probably be much different from mine. And I don't know how the situation would have turned out for sure since I'm not a lawyer. But this shows that if you don't make your wishes clear, you're leaving them open to interpretation, and your heirs could end up with unpleasant results.

This is precisely why you should talk to a skilled copyright attorney in addition to an estate attorney.

. . .

ANOTHER IMPORTANT (BUT STILL NEW) ELEMENT: DIGITAL ASSETS

A "digital asset" can be anything you use online, such as a social media account, online account, cryptocurrencies, photos, videos, music, and anything else that is intangible but important. Legally, digital assets generally refer to the right to access these items.

Digital assets are increasingly important in today's online age. I'll bet there are some very important photos on your phone right now that you might want to preserve. And everyone has online accounts —you can't survive without them.

If you had your will done before 2010, chances are that your attorney never thought about how important our online lives would be. This wasn't on my attorney's radar even in 2015.

But now, digital assets are critical. Some digital assets, like photos, have immense sentimental value

—few people use physical photo albums anymore, after all. Other digital assets, like e-books and music subscriptions, cannot be passed down because they're licensed and you don't own them. Every asset is unique and the nature of the digital assets you own will be much different from mine.

In the United States, many states have passed a version of the Revised Uniform Fiduciary Access to Digital Assets (RUFADAA) Act, which grants power to an executor to manage your online accounts and digital assets when you die. The laws also give certain protections to companies who provide online accounts.

However, it may be a good idea to include digital assets in your will so your wishes are clear. An attorney can help you with this, as requests for digital assets in wills are becoming more common. This trend will only continue, and if it's not yet common in your country, it will be eventually.

However, you'll also need to be aware of whether your online accounts provide "tools" for managing access to your account when you die. As we'll discuss later in the book, Apple, Facebook, and

Google offer tools that help you decide who gets access to your data after your passing. If a company offers a tool and you don't use it, then the company may not have to grant your executor access under the RUFADAA laws. Therefore, it's a smart strategy to use these tools whenever possible as long as there are no adverse consequences to your publishing business. We'll discuss this later in the book, but just make sure you talk to your attorney about including a digital assets provision in your will.

THE FINAL PITFALL: FINDING THE RIGHT ATTORNEY

I went to law school and I work regularly with counsel in my job, so I know how to talk to attorneys. I enjoy working with them and I understand how they think, which helped me a lot on my estate planning journey. If you don't have a legal background, you have to be really, really careful that you don't hire the wrong person.

When I began searching for an estate attorney, I had a hell of a time finding the right one. All of the attorneys I consulted with were good at their jobs and I could tell they knew their craft. However, none of them had worked with authors before, and they didn't know what to do with me. Some of them didn't take me seriously.

The personal parts of my estate are pretty simple, and any estate attorney can handle those. But as soon as I told them I was an author, I could almost see the confusion on their faces. As a client, I don't like that.

Attorneys are human just like the rest of us. They're just as capable of mistakes as anyone else. Except in your case, if your attorney makes a mistake, your heirs won't find out until you're dead. At that point, the attorney might be dead too. And if there's a mistake, your heirs are going to have to pay a law firm a lot of money to help, which is the exact opposite reason you hire an estate planning attorney in the first place.

Let me give you some examples of the struggles I encountered.

One attorney said that my copyrights were just like my other property, which is technically correct, but not in practice. This is exactly what my original estate lawyer told me, and you can see how that worked out.

Another attorney abruptly ended the call after I described my copyrights and said they couldn't help me. I at least appreciated their honesty.

One attorney told me that I was too young to be worried about my copyrights at this point in my life. That was incredibly insulting and misinformed.

Another attorney assured me they could handle my copyrights and then sent me a recommendation to do exactly what my original will did. If I wanted my original will, why would I have hired this person in the first place?

I went through at least a dozen attorneys before I found one who was willing to take the time to listen and understand my needs. I am very happy with the law firm I chose, and I am also happy with the service they provided me and my family. But my point is that I had to spend a lot of time and effort to find that firm.

You might have to search for a while too until you find the right person. Don't settle. Remember, as an author, you are not a typical client. Don't let an attorney try to convince you otherwise (unless they specialize in both estate planning and copyright, in which case you are a typical client).

If you can find an attorney who has worked with authors before, that's great, but if not, you may have to do what I did and retain a copyright attorney to help you. I always recommend that your estate attorney be located in the same town as you —it just makes things easier for your heirs. But your copyright attorney doesn't have to reside in your area. I found one in Chicago, where it is much easier to find specialized attorneys. If you live in a rural area or a small town, you may need to expand your geographic search to find a good copyright attorney.

I say these things not to paint attorneys in a bad light, but to give you some honesty that I wish someone had told me when I started my estate planning journey. It underscores that finding the right attorney who will understand you, listen, ask the right questions, and do right by your writing is the most critical thing you can do.

ACTION ITEMS

If you don't have a will, you're not serious about creating an author legacy. Here are some suggestions to get you started on the right path:

- Determine your last wishes and discuss them with all parties who will be in your will. Don't surprise anyone. The person you want to be your executor may not want the job. Make sure everyone agrees to serve your estate before moving forward.
- If you have a will, reread it. If it doesn't address your copyrights, rectify it ASAP.
- Whether you have a will or not, read a few

books on wills and trusts so you
understand the topic on more than a
superficial level. Even the best attorneys in
the world won't be able to help you if you
can't communicate your desires.

- Find a licensed estate attorney who
  specializes in wills and trusts in your area
  (hint: use Google). Find out if the attorney
  offers free consultations. If not, understand
  the attorney's price structures upfront so
  there are no surprises.
- Tell the attorney about your copyrights!
- Consider discussing a digital assets
  provisions in your will.
- Consult with a licensed copyright attorney
  in your area to double-check the estate
  attorney's work as it pertains to your
  copyrights. Or, choose a law firm that has
  both estate law and intellectual property as
  practice areas. This way your estate
  attorney can seek counsel in-house.
- Update your will after major life events,
  such as moving states, marriage, divorce,
  spousal death, the birth, coming of age,

marriage, or death of a child, the death or incapacitation of anyone listed in your will as a beneficiary, and other events that could impact how your personal and literary estate will pass to your heirs.

- Your attorney will give you several copies of your will. Separate them and keep them in a safe place that you and your heirs will remember. Destroy all copies of old wills.

YOUR LIVING WILL AND POWER OF ATTORNEY

We should also briefly discuss living wills. No discussion of wills and trusts would be complete without them because they create decisions that will be heavy for your heirs.

A last will and testament specifies your wishes after you die, but what happens if you end up in a coma and can't make decisions while you're alive?

A living will covers what you want to happen to you if you become incapacitated (such as in a coma). You specify what you want doctors to do if you have an incurable or irreversible condition that results in a state of permanent unconsciousness from which there is no reasonable medical certainty that you will recover. Do you want the doctors to prolong your life in hopes that you will make a long shot recovery, or do you want them to cease medical care?

In a living will, you designate power of attorney to someone to make decisions on your behalf if you become incapacitated. There are several different types of power of attorney (and not all of them are medical), but perhaps the most important is a medical power of attorney. A medical power of attorney makes healthcare decisions on your behalf. Depending on where you live, a living will and power of attorney may either be contained in the same document, or they may be addressed separately. If they are addressed together, they are known as an "advance directive."

In the United States, there was a media firestorm around the case of Terri Schiavo, a woman who ended up in a permanent vegetative state after a heart attack with almost no chance of recovery. She did not have a living will, so there was a fierce battle between her husband and her parents about whether her feeding tube should have been removed. What ensued was a long, protracted legal battle. Many Americans argued over this case at the dinner table for years. The country was deeply divided on the issue.

Terri Schiavo had her heart attack in 1990. When her husband finally succeeded in having her feeding tube removed (for the final time), Schiavo died in 2005. It took fifteen years in court to settle what could have been settled in an evening.

If you become incapacitated, the last thing you want before your death is fights between your heirs. A living will can eliminate that possibility. If your heirs are fighting while you're alive, just think about what kind of resentment and anger will exist after you're dead. Your author estate won't stand a chance.

The good news is that your attorney should draft a living will (and power of attorney) along with your last will and testament, so you can get them done at the same time. As long as you hire a good attorney, you should rest easy knowing that your medical wishes will be protected if you cannot make decisions for yourself.

TRUSTS

A trust is a legal entity that holds property and assets, and it manages them to the benefit of another party.

Trusts are complicated. There are DIY trust kits out there, but I wouldn't recommend them. I would only create a trust with an attorney's assistance. The person who creates a trust is a trustor (also known as a "grantor" or "settlor"). The trustor places property they own into the trust (called "funding" the trust), and the property is placed there for the benefit of the trust's beneficiaries, the people to whom the property will go when the trustor dies. A "trustee" manages the trust per the trustor's wishes. In many trusts, the trustor, beneficiary, and the trustee are the same person, at least until they die. Upon death, a "successor trustee" is appointed, who is usually the executor of the estate.

The trustor can use the trust to his or her benefit while they are alive. Then, when they die, for legal purposes, it's as if they never owned the property inside the trust. It's not uncommon to see land, vehicles, homes, and even companies placed into trusts. Trusts are commonly set up to pass property between generations. Trusts may also come with tax advantages.

A significant benefit of trusts is that property inside them does not have to go through probate. This means your heirs can access the property faster without having it go through probate court.

Also, when you consider that probate courts are public record in many countries, it's a big deal if you can keep your assets private. Some courts make wills available online.

There are many types of trusts.

A testamentary trust is a trust created by a will. It only goes into effect after you die. A testamentary trust must be probated, and it can increase your probate costs.

A living trust (also known as an inter vivos trust) is created while you are alive. You have far more control over a living trust which is why it may be better than a testamentary trust. Living trusts cost more money upfront, but many attorneys highly recommend them.

It's believed that the majority of living trusts ultimately fail because they are not set up or "funded" properly, even if you hire an attorney. You have to be careful and educate yourself on trusts if you go this route. They are not for the unorganized.

If an attorney does their job and you follow the strict rules of trusts, then you may be able to avoid probate entirely, or at least keep a significant amount of your estate out of probate. Otherwise, if your living trust fails, then you're going to have to hire an attorney to probate your estate anyway, which defeats the purpose.

There are many other types of living trusts depending on where you live. Trust types and purposes vary from country to country.

There are also many reasons to create a trust. Everyone's situation is different. What works for me may be a bad idea for you. You'll need to do your own research.

You might be contemplating whether it makes sense to place your copyrights into a trust, but I recommend talking to an estate attorney, a copyright attorney, and an accountant to determine whether you should place your copyrights into a trust, how, and when. In the United States, there could be unintended consequences for transferring copyrights to a trust while you're still alive. A lawyer can help you understand the pros and cons and how to orchestrate the treatment of your copyrights with your trust versus your will.

Just understand that trusts are not your only alternative for avoiding probate if you want to keep your copyrights out of court. In some cases, it may make sense to place your copyrights into a trust; or, it may make more sense to place them into your publishing LLC or corporation. Both can serve the same function. There's a lot to think about and there's no single answer that works for everyone, unfortunately. There are legal and tax consequences no matter what you decide.

So many factors go into trusts and I simply cannot give you any further information other than that you should consider it as a tool in your author estate.

Trusts are not cheap to set up. My revocable living trust cost me $1,500. After my will and power of attorney, my bill was over $2,000. I had to sacrifice to pay for the service, but I can rest easy knowing that my assets are protected when I'm gone.

ACTION ITEMS

- Determine if a trust is right for you and your family.
- If a trust is right for you, consult with an estate attorney and a copyright attorney to determine how a trust can help with your author estate.

OTHER FUNDAMENTALS

Let's talk about some other fundamentals in planning your estate.

LIFE INSURANCE

Life insurance is money that goes to your heirs after your death. You pay a premium and as long as your premium is paid and you don't violate any conditions of your policy, the company will send your family a check for the policy limits.

Life insurance can be expensive, but it's worth it. If you can afford it, I highly recommend it. Your heirs can use the money to settle debts, pay off your home, establish a college fund for children, or anything else that may be necessary. A former colleague of mine used her dad's life insurance money to make a down payment on her first home, something she wouldn't have been able to afford otherwise.

If you have a day job, your employer may offer a small amount of life insurance at a cheap rate (called "group life insurance" in Australia, Canada, and the United States, or "group life cover" in the UK). Group life shouldn't be your only life insurance policy because it terminates when your employment ends, but you can't beat the prices.

There are many types of life insurance. A financial adviser can help determine which types you should buy. My rule is to buy what you can afford. Something is better than nothing.

I can't write a book on estate planning without mentioning life insurance, so make sure you buy it for your family. It is a useful estate planning tool.

. . .

FIRE-RESISTANT SAFE

This should be an obvious tip, but you need safe places for all of your estate planning documents. I recommend at least one safe place in your home and one outside your home in case your home burns down or is destroyed.

Inside your home, I recommend a high-quality fire-resistant safe. They're frequently marketed as "fireproof safes," but just do a YouTube search to see how fireproof they are.

Your goal is to buy a high-quality **fire-resistant** safe. The best way to understand how a safe works is to read the label inside the door, like with mine:

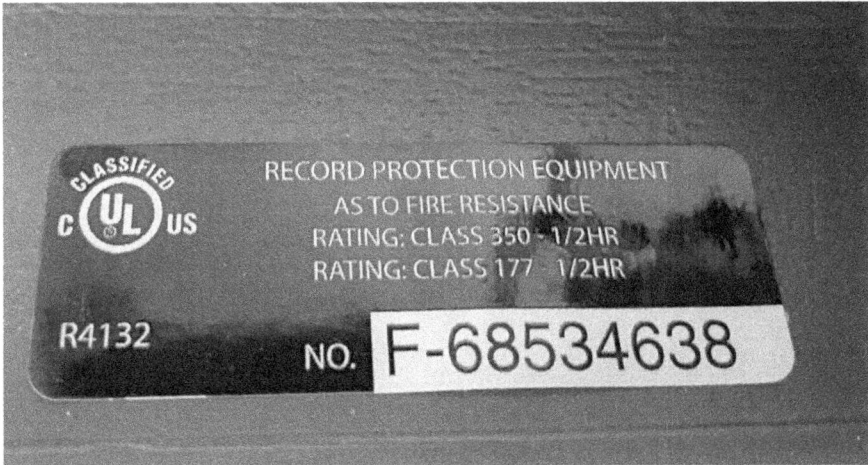

A quick Internet search shows that this safe adheres to the Underwriters Laboratory (UL) standard, which is considered by many to be the global gold standard. Another acceptable standard is KIS—Korean Industrial Standards.

The label contains a fire rating, which is the amount of time the interior of the safe will **resist** elevated temperatures associated with fire, but not fire itself.

The average house fire burns at approximately 1100 degrees Fahrenheit or 593 degrees Celsius. No safe will stand a chance if it is put into contact with direct flames. The best you can hope for is that the flames don't reach the safe so that it can withstand the hot temperatures in your home as it burns.

A Class 350 fire rating with 1/2 hour means that the inside of the safe will not exceed 350 degrees Fahrenheit or 177 degrees Celsius for 30 minutes. This rating is for paper products.

A Class 150 fire rating with 1/2 hour means that the inside of the safe will not exceed 150 degrees Fahrenheit or 66 degrees Celsius for 30 minutes. This rating is for electronic products such as flash drives or hard drives, as 150 degrees Fahrenheit is the point where they are ruined.

In other words, you're buying time with a safe in hopes that your local fire department will be able to extinguish the fire before your contents perish.

(If you noticed, the safe I bought is not suitable for electronics. I rectified that immediately after writing this chapter! I failed this fundamental step.)

Fire ratings are important because you'll need to purchase the correct-rated safe depending on your situation.

- Safes can be rated up to two hours. If you live in a rural area where the fire department can't respond to a fire immediately, a 30-minute rated safe is a waste of money.

- The bigger your house is, the longer it will burn.
- If you want to store other important items in the safe such as guns, then you'll need a special type of safe.
- Burglary safes won't help you in the event of a fire, and vice versa.

Fire-resistant safes may also come with water-resistant and burglar-resistant features as well. But, like with "fireproof" marketing, they may not be water- or burglar-proof either.

As an extra step, consider purchasing fire-resistant document bags to use with your fire-resistant safe. You can buy these relatively cheaply, and many are fire-rated as well. Look for ones with UL or KIS ratings and research the rating. Put your documents in the fire-resistant document bags, put the bags in your fire-resistant safe, and then hope for the best. Don't use bags alone, or your documents will burn.

Both fire-resistant safes and document bags are inexpensive and a smart investment.

If you use a fire-resistant safe, make copies of your key, and if the safe contains a passcode, write that passcode down and tell your heirs where they can find it. Otherwise, they'll have to break into the safe, which will cost money and possibly damage the contents inside.

SAFE DEPOSIT BOX

You can (and should) open a safe deposit box at your local bank. It's inexpensive and can serve as a safe place to store your documents if something were to happen to your home.

I recommend keeping copies of wills and other important documents in a safe deposit box. After all, we know that fire-resistant safes won't last that long in the event of a devastating fire. Bank safes, however, are engineered to be indestructible.

As safe as safes are, however, they may not be resistant to theft. There are news stories all the time of bank employees stealing the contents of safe deposit boxes, so be careful.

Also, don't keep your only copy of your estate planning documents in your box—otherwise, your heirs may have trouble accessing the box after your death, especially if they can't find the key.

If you sign up for a safe deposit box, make sure your heirs know it exists and how to get into it when you're gone. Read your deposit box agreement to learn how the bank handles your death, and keep the agreement outside of your safe deposit box!

Upon your death, the bank will usually require your executor to produce paperwork proving their relationship to you before granting them access. They may also seal your box unless they are court-ordered to open it, so make sure you understand their protocols while you're still alive so you can ensure easy access to the box after your death.

As a final tip, it is also wise to make an inventory of everything in your safe deposit box so your executor will know what's inside.

FINAL ARRANGEMENTS

What kind of funeral do you want to have (if you have one at all)? Which funeral home?

Do you want to be buried or cremated? Where?

If you want a gravestone, what do you want it to say? What kind of stone do you want it to be?

Maybe you want a family mausoleum or vault. Or maybe you want, as one of my grandmothers did, to donate your body to science.

You can make these decisions today and communicate them with your heirs.

Several years before his death, my grandfather prepaid all of his funeral expenses with a funeral home that he trusted. The family didn't have to pay any additional costs.

My in-laws are from Guatemala. They organized their burial arrangements and made it clear that they want to be buried in their home country. They purchased a plot in a cemetery where they will be buried. It'll be up to my wife and me to figure out how to expatriate their remains.

You don't have to prepay for your funeral expenses like my family, but you **can** decide how you want your final arrangements to be conducted. It will bring some comfort to your heirs when the time comes because they'll know that they're acting according to your wishes.

HELPFUL CONTACTS

Write down the contact information of service providers your executor will need after your death. They include but are not limited to your:

- chosen funeral home
- estate lawyer
- copyright lawyer

- financial adviser
- accountant
- life insurance company
- author/publishing friends who can lend a
  hand to your executor if they need help
  with the publishing or business side

This will be especially useful if your executor
doesn't live in your area. Do what you can to make
things easy for them, and never assume they'll be
able to figure it out.

ORGANIZING YOUR ESTATE

ESTATE ORGANIZATION BASICS

If you followed the steps in the previous chapter, then chances are high that you will have achieved the fundamentals. I trust that you will do the best you can to protect the personal part of your estate.

Now we move exclusively into **author** estate territory. This section will be where author estates will be made or broken. Even if you did all the fundamentals correctly, a single misstep in this section could undo your author legacy.

We must now figure out how to wrangle all the different pieces of running a writing business and organize them logically for our heirs to understand. Trust me when I say that this is an extremely painstaking task. But if you do it now, you'll be glad you did. As I said, no one is promised tomorrow.

Also, if you're diagnosed with a devastating disease, you might not have the capacity to do the things in this section later. Do them now while you can.

Many of these pieces may also correspond to your personal affairs. For example, if you're going to decide what to do with a business post office box, you should also figure out what to do with your personal mail. Keep that in mind as you read this section.

A HELPFUL ANALOGY

It's useful to think of your author business as an ecosystem.

An ecosystem has many elements, and each one plays a special part. If one element is disabled, it impacts other parts. If enough parts are damaged, the entire ecosystem collapses.

For example, take your bank account. When you die, your bank will eventually close your account. This means that book retailers won't be able to make direct deposits. If book retailers can't make direct deposits, they will send an email asking to update the bank information on file. But if your heirs don't have access to your email addresses or know which email addresses book retailers are communicating with, then your estate will collapse.

A good rule of thumb is that every element of your author business is connected to at least one other. This may not be immediately obvious to your heirs, so we have to help them understand the connections.

HELPING YOUR HEIRS BE SUCCESSFUL

. . .

Remember this phrase as you're organizing your estate: "Help your heirs A.I.M. for the stars."

A is for **Access**. To manage your estate, your heirs need access to everything (and I mean everything.)

I is for clear **Information**. Once your heirs have access, they need to understand how each element is used in your estate. If you have five email addresses, they need to know what each one is for. The same goes with multiple PayPal accounts. Never assume they'll be able to figure it out.

M is for **Management**. Once your heirs understand an element of your estate, they need to know how to manage it. Not all elements of your estate will be needed after your death; some accounts can be closed, for example. Other accounts, such as your hosting service, will be needed to keep your books discoverable.

When you help your heirs A.I.M. for the stars, they'll be able to access all your accounts with no limitations, know how each element of your author ecosystem works, and be able to manage it efficiently. As a result, they may be able to do more with your author estate after your death than you ever dreamed of during your lifetime. History is full of authors who saw little to no success while they were alive but who were phenomenally successful in death.

Anything can happen, so let's get prepared.

CATALOGING YOUR IP AND PHYSICAL PROPERTY

Before we do anything, I recommend taking an inventory of your intellectual property. Don't put your heirs in the unfortunate position of trying to figure out what you wrote. If you do, they could be finding copyrighted material from you for years, especially if you have a long career.

If you were a real estate landlord who owned many properties across the city, you wouldn't **not** write them all down, right?

It's the same with your copyrights. By creating an inventory, you're helping your heirs see a clear picture of what the estate owns.

Fortunately, cataloging your books is simple. Record:

- The title and subtitle of the book
- The author name or pseudonym
- The date published
- How you published it (traditional or self-published)
- Whether the book is exclusive to Amazon or not
- What formats the book is published in
- What the book is about (1-2 sentences)

Don't forget to describe the book! Just because you know what it's about doesn't mean your heirs will.

At a minimum, that's what I would start with. However, that's not really enough to run an estate. Consider creating a master publishing file that contains all the information about your books that your heirs will ever need. I learned this idea from fellow author estate expert M.L Buchman and I adapted it for my own purposes.

I wrote a book called **Keep Your Books Selling: Manage Your Book Portfolio and Make More Money**, and I include a free template in that book to help you set yours up.

My master publishing file includes:

- All the metadata for my books (title, subtitle, price, date published, ISBN, and much, much more)
- Links to the book on all retailers
- Production information such as the editor, cover designer, and dates
- License clearances (like the licenses for the images on the book cover)
- Format-specific metadata (I.e., paperback trim sizes, audiobook narrator details)

In other words, my master publishing file is a Swiss Army knife. It's amazing what I can do with it, it's easy to use, and it's heir-friendly.

If you've written a lot of books, expect the cataloging process to take a while. It took me about two weeks to catalog all of my intellectual property —and that was because I had to restart a few times in building my master file. However, you only have to do this once. Whenever you publish a new book, add the book to your publishing file.

BOOKS AREN'T THE ONLY IP YOU MAY OWN

Resist the urge to stop at your books. If you create short stories, blog posts, podcasts, or videos, then you also have additional intellectual property that needs to be cataloged. Any public speaking or public appearances also count as IP. How you catalog those items is up to you, but don't leave them out. Your heirs can leverage those copyrights too!

As a reminder, if you take the time to create an inventory now, you'll make your executor's work much easier when it's time to create an official inventory for probate.

DON'T FORGET YOUR PHYSICAL PROPERTY

Though the focus of this book is your intellectual property, you probably own physical property in the name of your publishing business. Items like computers, proof copies of paperbacks, credit card readers, webcams or cameras, keyboards, microphones, office supplies, are items you may have purchased to use for your writing operations. If your business bought it, you should inventory it.

ACTION ITEMS

- Create an inventory of all your intellectual property and keep it up-to-date.
- Create an inventory of all physical

property owned by your publishing
business.

THE SILVER BULLETS OF DOOM

There are several elements of your estate that if you get wrong, no amount of effort in the world will help your heirs. In fact, they won't be able to do virtually anything that I detail in this book. These elements are that important. If you successfully plan for them, you will be light-years ahead of other authors.

I call these dangerous elements "The Silver Bullets of Doom," and they are:

- Passwords and passcodes to your devices

- Usernames and passwords to your online accounts
- Two-factor authentication
- Email accounts
- Your book files
- Bank accounts
- Taxes
- Your domain(s) and your website(s)
- Your accounts with book retailers
- Scams

Why do I call them the Silver Bullets of Doom?

A "silver bullet" is used to describe something that succeeds instantly, usually in the context of werewolves. It is used in the positive sense, but in this book, I'm using it in the negative sense; if a Silver Bullet of Doom makes contact with your author estate, it will dismantle it instantly. A blow from any one of these bullets is instant death.

In other words, you can follow all the tried-and-true estate planning advice, but if you make one mistake in this section and your estate gets hit by one of these bullets, your hard work may not matter.

In researching this book, I tried to find out what happened to several self-published authors who died recently—if their books were still available, and if their estates were active. Not one of them had even a minimal online presence anymore. I don't know for sure, but I'd guess that the Silver Bullets of Doom had something to do with it.

I will help you understand the Silver Bullets of Doom and the pitfalls associated with them. Some of the pitfalls aren't immediately obvious, but some are so obvious that they're invisible. You may not even be aware of them until I point them out.

Better to realize problems now than for your heirs to discover them after you're dead!

PASSWORDS TO YOUR DEVICES AND APPS

I shouldn't have to write this, but make sure your heirs know how to access your devices.

If your heirs are your spouse and children, they probably know where your writing computer is. They also will know where your phone is.

But if your heirs don't live with you or live far away, they may not know. And if you protect your computer or phone with a password or passcode—well, the Silver Bullet of Doom is coming for you.

This also includes any apps you use with a password, like…a writing app.

Again, this should be painfully obvious, but I have to say it because there will inevitably be many people who read this chapter who have never written their device passwords down. I can say that authoritatively because I myself didn't start doing it until I wrote this book…

Here's how to solve this problem once and forever: get an index card, write down the name of your devices, and any associated passwords or passcodes.

Keep the index card on your desk where your heirs can see it, or tape it to the back or bottom of your desk if you want a little more privacy, or put it in a fire-resistant safe, or deliver it to your bank safe deposit box, or give it to your loved ones along with other estate essentials. Whatever you do, tell your heirs!

If you handwrite the information, do it as if your fifth-grade teacher is going to read it. Make sure your handwriting is as clear as possible.

Finally, make sure that you update the index card whenever you change your passwords or passcodes.

I suspect far too many writers have died without leaving their computer password information, making their devices inoperable, therefore cutting their heirs off entirely from their book files and any chance of recovering online accounts.

Fortunately, this Silver Bullet of Doom is the easiest to dodge.

ACTION ITEMS

- Write down your passwords and passcodes for your devices and tell your heirs where to find them.

USERNAMES AND PASSWORDS TO ONLINE ACCOUNTS

You don't need me to tell you that usernames and passwords are important. Your heirs need them to access your accounts. Everyone knows this, yet few people take steps to ensure that their passwords are accessible in the event of an untimely death.

According to Dashlane, a password manager company, the average person has 150 online accounts. If you have a writing business, you will have well over that amount. Can you remember all of those passwords? Probably not.

If you're one of the millions of people who use the same password on all of your accounts, I highly recommend that you stop doing that. It might be convenient, but it is unsafe and will expose you to hacking attacks.

A few times a year, there's always a story on a major media outlet about a company whose usernames and passwords were stolen by hackers. Invariably, the users whose accounts were breached had easy-to-guess passwords, like "password" or "123456." It's funny, but people still do it even though they know the risks.

Cyber security best practices dictate that you should have a strong password that includes lower- and upper-case letters, numbers, symbols, and a reasonable character length, usually no less than 10 characters.

But you're probably thinking, "I can't remember passwords if I use a different one on every site!" And you're correct.

Your first inclination might be, as many do, to write your usernames and passwords down in a notebook that you keep on your desk, but that's inconvenient. It's also not secure if your home is burglarized. If your home burns down or is lost in a catastrophe such as a tornado or a flood, you'll lose all your passwords.

So, what do we do?

I strongly recommend a password manager. A password manager is a secure digital vault that helps you to safely and conveniently store all of your login credentials. It also automatically fills in your username and passwords for you. Popular password managers include 1Password, LastPass, Dashlane, and Bitwarden.

Here's how you enter a password without a password manager:

- Go to the website and click Login.
- Remember the username and password.
- If you can't remember the password, consult your notebook or a digital file that has all your passwords, which takes time.
- Enter your username and password correctly.
- If you don't remember the username or password, you have to click the "Forgot

Username or Password" button and follow the steps, which is a hassle.

Here's how logging in with a password manager works:

- Go to the website and click Login.
- Your password manager autofills your username and password.
- You're in.

If you ever change your username or password, the manager will update it automatically. If you create a new account, the password manager will store it for the next time you need to log in.

(And yes, I recognize that browsers can store your login information, but they're not secure. If someone gets access to your Google account, for example, they will also inherit your passwords if you use Chrome. It's not safe!)

Password managers also sync between your devices, so you have access to your passwords no matter what device you are on. Major password managers can be used with any operating system and any browser.

They are reasonably priced too. I pay around $40 per year for 1Password.

I use 1Password to generate very long, difficult passwords, and I keep them in my vault. I have a master password that gets me into the vault. I only have to remember one password, and it has been ages since I have had to click that "Forgot Password" button. I can't tell you how much time I have saved over the years NOT having to remember passwords.

Perhaps the best security feature that password managers offer is emergency access. With this feature, you grant emergency access to a designated person. For example, if I happen to get locked out of my account, I can use a trusted contact who will get instant access to the vault so I can reset my master password. You can use this feature with your heirs; if you designate an heir to have instant access to your account if you die unexpectedly, they can get in immediately and recover all of your passwords!

Password managers also allow you to group accounts into categories and folders as an estate planning tool. For example, I organize my accounts based on what should happen to them when I die. One folder contains subscriptions that need to be canceled immediately upon my death, and another contains the subscriptions that need to be continued. I update the folders to reflect changes at least twice per year. This way, my executor knows quickly what actions need to be taken.

With a password manager, I enjoy secure passwords, the convenience of being able to autofill them in my desktop and phone browsers, and the peace of mind that my heirs will have access to everything.

If you use a password manager correctly, you will almost certainly dodge the first Silver Bullet of Doom.

If you have concerns about storing all of your passwords in one place, you are justified. After all, if someone gets your master password, then they have all of your passwords. However, you can secure your password manager with two-factor authentication so that if someone guesses your master password, they still can't get into your account. We will discuss two-factor authentication in the next chapter.

My opinion is that the convenience and security of a password manager are superior to using one password on all of your sites (or writing them down on paper). Even if someone were to guess your master password, they still can't get into your account if you use two-factor authentication correctly.

If you are using the same password everywhere, if someone guesses one password, they now have them all. You probably won't have a clue that a breach happened, or which of your accounts are vulnerable. Operating without a password manager is far riskier in my opinion.

At least with a password manager, if one of your accounts is hacked, your liability is limited to that password. You can regenerate a new one to secure your account, and you'll know that your other accounts are safe because they all have different passwords.

If you're still leery about the security of a password manager and won't take my word for it, then consider that many IT and cybersecurity professionals strongly recommend them too. Do some research on them and check them out for yourself.

I recommend 1Password or LastPass. I have used and enjoyed both services. 1Password has a better track record of security and more features. LastPass has had some security vulnerabilities in recent years, and many people are moving away from it, but it's still a very good password manager.

In any case, whether you use a password manager or not, you still need to store your passwords in a place where your heirs can find them.

The requirements for granting access to your passwords correctly for your heirs include:

- Gathering all of your passwords
- Keeping them up-to-date
- Keeping them in a place your heirs can find them

Using a password manager accomplishes all of these goals with little to no effort. You can also use a "Notes" field in the password manager to describe what each of your accounts is used for, which will help your heirs A.I.M. for the stars.

If you use pen and paper or another way, you'll have to be creative. If you write your passwords down, you have to be very, very careful to update your notebook any time you change a password. Failing to do so could be catastrophic.

In case I need to remind you just how catastrophic bungling your passwords can be, consider the following scenarios:

- You're "all-in" and exclusive to Amazon via its Kindle Direct Publishing Select program (KDP Select). You forgot to leave your heirs your Amazon password, so they are forever locked out of your Amazon account. When your bank learns of your death, it will pay your beneficiaries any money in the account and then close it. Amazon will then have no bank account to pay sales commissions to, effectively cutting off your heirs forever.

- Your book files are stored in the cloud. If your heirs want to make an update to one of your books or upload it to a new place, they cannot because they cannot access the book files.

- After your death, the government decides to audit your tax return. It sends a threatening letter to your heirs questioning them about several business expenses you made. Because you use online accounting software but didn't leave your password, your heirs have no way of fighting the audit and your estate gets assessed additional taxes.

- Your heirs check your email one morning and discover that a significant amount of money has been deposited into your PayPal account, but they can't access your PayPal account because PayPal will not release account information even to executors or heirs. The money is forever gone.

- Your credit card on file at various websites expires several years after your death, and your heirs can't log in to update it. Therefore, all services you paid for expire. Among those are your website hosting provider and your PPC service (like Amazon or Facebook ads). Any hope you have of sales is finished.

Now, imagine all of those scenarios happening at the same time. Failing to leave passwords will have many additional unforeseen ramifications that will culminate in the literal death of your author estate. It will be a long, agonizing death, and quite painful for your heirs, especially if they need the income that your books generate.

You might be thinking, "But if my executor provides legal documents and a death certificate, a company has to grant them access!"

Companies like Google and Facebook give you options on how you want their data to be handled after death. However, if you elect not to exercise those options, that's on you. Wish your heirs good luck convincing Facebook and Google's attorneys to let them in. They'll never even be able to get someone on the phone.

In a previous chapter on wills, we talked about how many states in the United States have passed digital fiduciary laws, but the fine print in the laws is that companies and users are still governed by terms of service. Just because the law gives power to your executor, it doesn't necessarily mean that companies have to grant login credentials.

I wouldn't count on smaller companies providing login information either. Small companies in particular go to great lengths to protect user privacy because of reputational risk.

Be kind to your heirs. Don't let them go down this path. It's a cruel thing to do to them.

The bottom line is that you have to have a strategy for storing your passwords, and you have to store them in a place your heirs can access quickly. Don't be one of the many writers whose passwords die with them. There is no recovery from this type of error.

A final issue I'll point out is that even though you give your passwords to your heirs, that doesn't mean you've solved the problem. There's still the issue of account ownership. As one prominent estate attorney on YouTube put it, your passwords are just the keys to the account, just like the keys to a car. Just because I give you the keys to my car, that doesn't mean you own it.

Preserving passwords is always a smart strategy, but you'll want to discuss how to transition account ownership with your attorney. This is an area where companies differ wildly, and what you can and can't do may depend on where you live and what the laws are in your area. We'll cover this for publishing accounts specifically later in the book.

ACTION ITEMS

- Use a password manager to gather and store your passwords in a safe place.
- Secure the password manager with two-factor authentication using an authenticator app and a physical security key.

- Store your master password in a safe place.
- Use the password manager's emergency access feature to grant immediate access to an heir upon your death. This is extra insurance in case they cannot find your master password.

TWO-FACTOR AUTHENTICATION

At the time of this writing, two-factor authentication (also known as 2FA, two-step verification, multifactor authentication, or MFA) is a relatively new security feature that requires a user to enter a second proof of identification to access an account.

With traditional logins, you have to enter a username and password to access an account. With two-factor authentication, you have to enter your username and password **and** verify that you are the owner using an additional method. Usually, that method is a one-time passcode that is sent via text message or email. The code is time-sensitive.

Many banks require 2FA as an additional security measure, but most companies do not require it. At the time of this writing, you usually have to opt-in for it.

I strongly recommend that you use 2FA to secure your accounts to give yourself added security while you're alive. It is designed to be foolproof, and with a few exceptions, it is. You may be using 2FA on some of your accounts already.

Another potential danger you should be aware of is identity theft after death. Cyber thieves troll obituaries and death records to look for easy prey. They can file tax returns under your name, open bank accounts, and wreak all sorts of havoc that your heirs will have to clean up. If you don't follow cyber best practices while you're alive, you will be defenseless after you're dead.

Consider that as an author, you're a public figure, and if you've achieved some success, there may be some publicity about your death so that people can pay tribute to you. That's a prime opportunity for a thief to look for accounts to hack into—no one's going to be paying attention because they'll be busy grieving, after all. 2FA keeps you protected.

However, if you do use 2FA in any capacity, be very careful. If not, your heirs will be locked out of your accounts even if they have your usernames and passwords.

That's why 2FA is a Silver Bullet of Doom. You may be required to use it already on some sites, and more sites may require it in the future. You will not be able to get around this problem.

Most people right now are using their phones for 2FA, which is dangerous in several non-obvious ways. I bet you have received those text message passcodes again and again and never once thought about how screwed your heirs could be if they don't have access to your phone. If something happens to your phone while you're alive, you'll be locked out of your accounts until you can buy a replacement. If you die and your heirs disconnect your phone without understanding 2FA, they'll be locked out of your accounts forever.

At this juncture, you have a critical question to answer: are you using 2FA today in any capacity?

If the answer is no, the next critical question is whether you should. If you choose not to, fine.

If the answer is yes, then you may have an existential threat to both your personal and author estates. You must read this chapter and you must make sure you understand it. 2FA is not difficult, but some people may find it a little too technical and "techy." I won't deny that.

If 2FA doesn't make sense after reading this chapter, I recorded two short videos so you can see it in action. I'll link to them at the end of this chapter.

Please note that failure to take steps to address the 2FA problem may doom your author legacy. If I sound overly alarmist, it's because I don't believe enough authors understand how much danger 2FA is to their estates. I predict that too many people are going to learn the hard way. This chapter will open your eyes to just how problematic 2FA can be, and how you can address the problem safely.

Now that I've rung the alarm bells enough, let's turn them off and talk about the different types of two-factor authentication methods.

TEXT MESSAGE (SMS) AUTHENTICATION

With text message authentication, the company sends you a text message with a one-time passcode that you must enter after inputting your password. This is also known as SMS authentication. To validate your account, you must have your phone nearby. Your phone serves as your key.

SMS 2FA is the most common verification method, but it is the least secure because of an attack hackers can use called "SIM Swapping." In a SIM swap attack, a hacker calls your cell phone provider and pretends to be you. They convince your provider to switch your phone number to a different SIM card. Then, when they log in to your accounts with your username and password, they receive the one-time passcode to their phone.

The chances of a SIM swapping attack are rare for most people, but it could happen.

There's another better reason not to use your phone for two-factor authentication that I mentioned previously: if something happens to your phone, you won't be able to receive text messages until you find a replacement. When you die, your phone number will eventually be terminated. What happens, for instance, if you die and your heirs disconnect your phone without realizing that they need it to authenticate your accounts? Uh oh.

Even if your heirs keep your phone active for a time, they're going to have to cancel it at some point. That's why SMS authentication is a bad idea. Yet, at the time of this writing, many companies only offer SMS authentication, which makes the issue more difficult. Cyber security professionals have been urging companies to move away from SMS authentication for the reasons I mentioned in this section, but companies are reluctant to do so.

MOBILE PROMPT AUTHENTICATION

. . .

Some companies such as Google rely on an app that already exists on your phone to authenticate your account.

For example, at the time of this writing, Google will ask you to open a Google app on your phone such as YouTube. When you do, a code will appear in the YouTube app and you have to match that to the code in the account where you are trying to log in.

These types of prompts are tied to your phone number. As with SMS authentication, if your phone is lost, you can't authenticate, which will lock your heirs out of your accounts.

EMAIL AUTHENTICATION

Instead of an SMS notification, you can elect to have your one-time passcode sent to your email address, which is much safer, but not 100 percent secure if your email accounts are ever breached.

However, email authentication is much better than SMS because if something happens to your phone, you can access your email from any device that has an Internet connection. If you secure your email address with a strong password and two-factor authentication (for your email account itself), then it is a safe way to authenticate your accounts. Logging in to your email may be less convenient than receiving a text message, but it's still a good way to protect yourself.

Also, it's worth pointing out that if your heirs don't have access to your email accounts, then you're relegating them to doom because they'll never be able to pass 2FA for any other account you have.

APP AUTHENTICATION

You can also authenticate your account using a dedicated authenticator app. Examples include Google Authenticator, Authy, and Microsoft Authenticator. I use and recommend Authy.

All authenticator apps are free and they work the same way: they generate one-time passcodes for your accounts and change them every 30 seconds. You log in to your desired account with your username and password, open your authenticator app, grab the code, and you're in.

At first glance, authenticator apps usually scare people off because they look way too complicated, but they're not. They're not immediately intuitive, though.

To set up any authenticator app, the steps are the same:

- Go to your account dashboard, enable two-factor authentication, and then select the authenticator app option. You will see a QR code appear on the screen.
- Open your authenticator app, select "Add Account," and that will activate your QR scanner. Scan the code.
- In your authenticator app, you will then be given a one-time passcode that expires in

30 seconds. Enter the code in your desired account to complete the authentication.

- The next time you log in and are asked for the code, open your authenticator app to get it.

The major benefit of authenticator apps is that they can be used on both desktop and mobile devices. This means that if you pick the right one, you won't be married to your phone for codes.

Some password managers such as 1Password also allow you to generate one-time passcodes within the app. You'll see it next to your password. However convenient this is, this is less secure because if someone hacks your password manager, they can get your codes too. It's probably safer to use a separate authenticator app.

The authenticator app I recommend is Authy. Authy works on both your desktop and phone, and it allows you to sync your account between devices. This means that if anything were to happen to your phone, you can still get the one-time passcode on a computer. Your codes are stored in the cloud, which could be a concern for some, but they are encrypted on your computer before they're sent to the cloud, so you have pretty good security.

Security experts don't recommend using cloud backups for 2FA, but the small tradeoff in security is worth it for one important reason: your heirs can install Authy on their computer, link your account, and start getting the codes right away. It's very, very useful, and it will get heirs around this Silver Bullet of Doom.

I recommend an authenticator app as your primary or secondary 2FA method.

PHYSICAL SECURITY KEY AUTHENTICATION

If you want the best security of all, you can buy a physical USB security key. After you enter your username and password, you insert your security key into a USB port on your computer or the charging port on your phone. Some sensors require you to tap the key or scan your fingerprint to authenticate your account.

The image below is a YubiKey 5C NFC. You insert this into a USB-C slot and then tap the gold button on the key to authenticate. It fits easily on a necklace or a key ring too.

Physical security keys are considered to be the safest authentication method because hackers can't fool them. They also can't replicate them digitally. A hacker would have to hack your accounts and steal your security key, which is next to impossible.

There's another good reason to use a security key. Sometimes, hackers can use a trick called "spoofing." With a spoofing attack, the hackers create fake websites that look eerily similar to the real ones, such as a bank's website. They lure you to the website by sending you an email or text pretending to be the company you trust. If you enter your credentials, they'll steal your login info. A security key can detect spoofs because it scans the website domain. It will only work on the real version of the website, therefore frustrating hackers and alerting you to the fact that you were fooled. You can then immediately change your password and report the attack.

You can also take security keys with you everywhere you go. They're small enough to fit on a keychain, in a wallet, or on a necklace.

I recommend the YubiKey brand. There are many models to suit your needs, but most IT and cybersecurity professionals agree that these are the best security keys on the market. Another prominent security key model is Google Titan.

On a desktop or laptop, you can leave your security key in a USB port so that you don't have to insert it every time you need to authenticate your accounts. As long as the key is in the port, you'll enjoy near-automatic authentication.

On a phone, security keys are a little more cumbersome, but not very. You will have to insert the security key into your charging port every time authentication is needed. However, some keys support near-field communication (the same technology that powers Apple Pay and Google Pay), and you can tap the key on the back of the phone to authenticate, which is much more convenient.

I paid around $50 for each of my security keys. New models are coming out all the time, so research the one that is best for you.

If you buy a security key, buy at least two: one as your primary, and another as a backup that you keep in a fire-resistant safe or safe deposit box. You can link both to your accounts. Most places that accept security keys allow you to link an unlimited number of keys to your account. This way, your heirs can use any of your keys.

Security keys aren't well-supported right now, but I expect that to change in the future.

. . .

BACKUP CODES

Some providers give you one-time backup codes to use in case you are locked out of your account. These are the option of last resort, but useful if you ever need them.

If a company gives you backup codes, store them in a safe place. Write them down or put them in a password-protected file. Don't be the person who doesn't write them down and then needs them someday!

SECURING TWO-FACTOR AUTHENTICATION FOR YOUR HEIRS

At the time of this writing, not every website supports 2FA. Not every site supports it equally either.

Most banks don't support authenticator apps or hardware keys yet, so you're forced to use SMS.

Some sites like Adobe only allow SMS and email authentication.

Other sites, like Google, Facebook, and Amazon allow for all authentication methods.

As a result, if you use 2FA, you're likely using a patchwork of different methods, which is the biggest drawback right now.

My 2FA strategy is to use physical security keys as my primary method wherever and whenever possible, and an authenticator app as my secondary method. If absolutely necessary, I will use email authentication. I disable SMS at any place that will let me. I'm betting on authenticator apps and security keys enjoying better support in the future. I may be wrong, but at least I know I'm taking the best steps to secure my accounts.

Your strategy could look like mine, or it could be more conservative, with you enabling as many 2FA methods as possible to maximize your heirs' chances of recovering your accounts. It's up to you.

It's not enough just to use 2FA while you're alive. You must also be thoughtful about how your heirs will get your passcodes.

WHERE TO START

It doesn't matter whether you like 2FA and use it regularly or if you actively avoid it. Chances are high that you're using it somewhere, and you need to document where. Otherwise, your heirs will be locked out of your accounts.

Use a site like the 2FA Directory to determine which sites support 2FA. Go through the list slowly and write down the websites where you have accounts. Don't rely solely on your memory; you may forget one or two websites and that could be troublesome for your heirs. Some password managers like 1Password can also alert you to which companies support 2FA.

Also, go through your favorite bookmarks to see if there are any additional sites where you use 2FA.

Create a password-protected spreadsheet that records how you're addressing 2FA. I've created a template for you at www.authorlevelup.com/2FAtemplate. Modify it as you see fit. I also have an Estate Plan Organizer Excel sheet that I'll share at the end of this book that also includes a tab for 2FA.

Next, go to each website and determine which 2FA methods they support, and which ones you are willing to use. Record the website and mark which methods you are using on the spreadsheet. If the service offers backup codes, create a separate tab on the worksheet and paste your codes there.

As an obvious reminder, you'll also need to update the spreadsheet any time you create a new account that supports 2FA.

Next, password-protect the spreadsheet and store the password both in your password manager and in your fire-resistant safe or safe deposit box.

Creating this spreadsheet will be a pain, but it's the best way of getting your heirs around the two-factor authentication problem that I can think of.

Otherwise, you're forcing them to guess where you've used 2FA and you're increasing the chances that they won't be able to find your codes. Remember, we've got to help our heirs A.I.M. for the stars!

Also, consider imparting some strong words to your heirs: **Under no circumstances** should your phone line be disconnected until all 2FA websites have authentication disabled or have been updated with a new phone number that your heirs will have access to. Otherwise, they could be cutting themselves off from your accounts.

FINAL THOUGHTS

When used with a password manager, two-factor authentication will maximize your security with:

- secure passwords that are difficult for hackers to guess
- passcodes that hackers won't have access to

2FA isn't the most convenient thing in the world to use, but it's critical. Many experts say that you should enable it on your email accounts, bank accounts, and other sensitive financial or health accounts at a minimum. I recommend adding it to any account you have that provides it, especially your writing-related accounts.

Two-factor authentication is a must-have in today's digital world. Not every website supports it, and most that do allow it to be optional. As cyberattacks continue, more websites will change their stance. Try if you want, but you won't be able to get around this problem even if you actively avoid 2FA.

At the time of this writing, few writing-related websites even offer it. Amazon and Draft2Digital are the first that come to mind. Expect more retailers to offer it in the coming years, either as a result of a security breach or because of user demand.

If you still need help understanding how 2FA works, I've created two short videos to help you see it visually:

- Two-Factor Authentication Explained in Three Minutes
- How to Set Up an Authenticator App in Three Minutes

You can watch the videos at www. authorlevelup.com/2FAvideos.

EMAIL

The third Silver Bullet of Doom is perhaps the most deceptive.

You should, of course, record the usernames and passwords of every email account you own. If you followed the steps in the last two chapters, you're covered. But there are other unusual problems endemic to email accounts that can cause trouble for your heirs.

I've read that the average person has 1.75 email accounts. As an author, you are likely to have far more.

. . .

WHAT HAPPENS TO YOUR EMAIL ACCOUNTS WHEN YOU DIE

If you've never read the terms of service for the email clients you use, now is a very good time to do so.

Since many people use Google Mail (Gmail) as their email provider, let's take a look at their terms.

Google has a master terms of service that applies to your entire Google account, with each Google service having its separate terms.

Here's the first applicable Gmail term that applies to your death: "Use the product to remain active. Activity includes accessing the product or its content at least every [two] years. We may take action on inactive accounts, which may include deleting your messages from the product." Additionally, another clause states, "If you're over your [storage] quota for [two] years or longer… [and] if you don't free up or purchase more space to get back under quota, all of your content may be removed from [Google]."

In plain English, Google is reserving the right to delete your account after two years of inactivity or if you exceed your email storage quota for over two years. This means that all of your Google data will be deleted within two years of your death if your heirs do nothing or are locked out.

(If you publish directly to Google Play and/or have a YouTube channel that is making money, this is particularly problematic. More on those later.)

Google does give you a release valve in the event you lock your heirs out of your account. You can use its Inactive Manager to designate who will receive your Google data **before** they delete your account. This person will receive all your Google data from many (but not all) of your Google products, which could be many, many gigabytes' worth of data, including your emails.

(A better way than making your heirs wait two years, however, would be to make sure they have access to your Google accounts.)

No matter what they do, your heirs have two years, maybe less before Google takes action. I suppose your heirs could continue using your account, which would add more time to the clock, but it would be wise if you instructed them to, wherever necessary, change the email address at any places you may anticipate receiving email from. Otherwise, here's what will eventually happen:

- Google will terminate your account, including your Gmail (and Google Play Partner Center).
- Any accounts that have your Gmail account as the registered address or username will no longer have a valid email address on file, which means companies cannot send notifications of issues that arise with your account (like a problem with a royalty payment).
- Your heirs won't get important emails, and that could have unintended consequences, including lost income.

See why I say that email is part of the Silver Bullets of Doom?

And that's just Google. If you use another popular email provider, you'll need to review their terms. Some email providers say that your account will (technically) terminate upon your death. Google's terms are quite generous in comparison.

In any case, the clearest instructions you can give to your heirs is to change your email addresses on file with all important accounts as soon as possible after your death. They can easily identify affected accounts with a password manager. Then, they should use the tips I suggest later in the chapter (combining inboxes and forwarding) to monitor your email account until it is deleted.

If I were your heirs, I would not proactively delete an email account because you never know what emails might arrive. I'd keep any email addresses open as long as possible, and unless your terms of service require you to disclose it or forbid others to use your account on your behalf, you may want to delay a death notification to the email provider as long as possible. (But you need to read your email app's terms and possibly talk to your attorney on whether you can do this.)

. . .

GATHER EVERYTHING (AND I MEAN EVERYTHING)

The most important thing you can do is track down all email addresses you have or could have had at any time. This includes both personal and business emails.

You probably have a primary address that you use for most communications, and at least one secondary email address. I know some people who have dozens of email addresses.

The problem with numerous email accounts is that your heirs won't know where your emails are going. They may not even know why you have certain accounts, or that those accounts exist. If you forget to tell them about a certain email address, and an important email goes to that address...your heirs won't have access.

Why is this important? There are many important emails that your heirs may need to contend with:

- two-factor authentication emails
- important updates regarding one of your accounts, such as a credit card expiration, a data breach, or a time-sensitive requirement to do something, like agree to updated terms of service
- sales commission reports from retailers
- royalty reports from publishers
- receipts or product keys
- emails from your readers telling your heirs that something is wrong in one of your books or on your website
- fan mail from your readers
- opportunities from Hollywood or other rights buyers who want to offer your heirs money to adapt your work

The point is that you have no idea what kind of emails will be sent to you after you die. The more accounts you have, the higher the chances that something will be lost in transit.

Consider my story. At the time of this writing, I have:

- a personal email.
- a "professional" email for my insurance career; I use it when applying for jobs, corresponding with recruiters, and so on.
- a "burner" email address that I use for sites where I don't want to give my preferred email address.
- a separate email for my YouTube channel so I can manage those emails cleanly.
- and more.

But that's not all. I also have email addresses associated with my domain names.

Email marketing best practices dictate that a sender's address should come from a domain-level address. If you use an email marketing service like Mailchimp to send emails to readers with your Yahoo or Gmail address as the sender, your delivery rates will suffer. So, you have no choice but to create a domain email.

On the domain side, I have:

- A "domain" email address that I use

mainly to improve my email marketing deliverability.

- A "contact" email address that I use for contact forms. I have hired VAs to help manage my emails in the past, and I believe giving them a dedicated email address looks more professional to readers.

To review, that's at least seven email addresses I have to manage.

To make matters worse, I haven't always been consistent with which email address I use to sign up for accounts, magnifying the problem even more.

If you're anything like me, you have way more email addresses than the average person, and you must address this problem now.

COMBINING YOUR EMAIL INBOXES

If you are fairly tech-savvy, my advice in this section will already be familiar to you.

However, if you are not tech-savvy, and if you are logging in to each of your email accounts individually, stop. That will make things too complicated for your heirs.

I recommend that you use an email client that supports combining email accounts. Email combination simply means that you can access all of your inboxes from one app at the click of a button.

The app I use is Airmail, but there are dozens upon dozens of different choices. Microsoft Outlook also supports this feature. I can import common accounts like Gmail or Yahoo easily, and I can also import domain-related addresses with a few steps.

In my email client, I receive all the emails from the accounts I mentioned previously in one place. I can toggle between inboxes whenever I want to. Whenever I send an email, I can choose which email address I'm sending it from. The email client will update the signature accordingly.

Email combination makes your life so much easier, and your heirs will thank you for it. When you die, you just need to tell them where to find your email app, then they'll be able to see all of your emails in one place. With a bit of help, they'll also be able to figure out how to combine your emails with the email inboxes they already use.

An alternative to an email combination that can be just as effective is email forwarding. Instead of checking each email account separately, you can set your secondary addresses to forward to your primary address. For example, any email that goes to your secondary address will automatically be forwarded to your primary. You can usually specify whether you want forwarded emails to be deleted or whether you want to keep a copy.

Email forwarding may be a little simpler for your heirs because they just need to access your primary email address. However, combining your email inboxes is more transparent and it will be easier to spot issues if they arise. If one of your addresses stops forwarding, your heirs may not know right away, whereas most email clients would notify them immediately if email combination stops working.

The choice is up to you, but at least talk to your heirs about it, and tell them how they will access your emails after you die.

WHERE TO START

Let's start with three easy steps.

First, inventory all of your emails. Close any email accounts you are not actively using. Streamline your email accounts now to minimize future work for your heirs.

Second, unsubscribe from marketing emails with extreme prejudice. Anything you can do to eliminate your email volume will be helpful in the long run.

Third, for the email accounts you wish to keep, confirm that you can log in, and secure them by recording them into your password manager with strong passwords. Then enable two-factor authentication and record which methods you use as well as any backup codes.

These first three steps will ensure that your heirs will have access.

Next, determine whether you should combine your email inboxes or forward secondary email accounts to your primary. Your strategy may involve a mixture of both. My strategy, for example, is to combine email inboxes from common providers like Gmail but to forward domain-related accounts because I don't use those very often.

When you're done, you'll ensure that your heirs will have access to your email accounts, receive ALL your emails, and be able to access those emails in the way that is most convenient for them.

A FINAL STEP

This section is entirely optional, but you may find it useful.

If your website has a contact form, tell your heirs not to delete it!

As I wrote previously, I would strongly recommend keeping email channels open because you never know when an opportunity could come to your heirs.

Consider drafting an autoresponder for your contact form. An autoresponder is a message that a sender receives immediately after sending an email to your email address.

In your autoresponder, consider letting the sender know that you've passed away but that someone from your estate will be in touch. I would politely explain that certain types of questions simply cannot be answered anymore. As a thank you, give them a coupon code to buy a book from you directly, with a link to your store. (But if you do this, make sure to disclaim that you can't promise the code will be available forever, so they should act now. That way, if it doesn't work, they'll have some grace with you. You're dead, after all.)

If a reader sees an email like that, they might become a fan for life. They certainly won't pester your estate either. And it just might improve your book sales.

. . .

ACTION ITEMS

- Read the terms of service for all email providers you use, and take care not to breach any terms when planning your estate.
- Inventory your email addresses for your executor along with usernames and passwords. Record what each email address is used for, how frequently you check it, and how you access it (i.e., by logging in to each account individually or using an email client on your desktop or phone).
- Inventory which of your online accounts use that email address. Your heirs will need to change the email address on file at all your online accounts after your death. (Hint: use a password manager to skip this step.)
- Read your email provider's terms of service. If you use Google, visit their

Inactive Manager and designate a beneficiary for your data once your account is deleted after your death.

- Delete any email accounts you do not need.
- Unsubscribe from as many email lists as you can and find ways to reduce your email volume.
- Consider combining your email inboxes with an email client and/or setting up forwarders for secondary email addresses so that your heirs will be able to access all future emails in one place.
- Consider setting up an autoresponder "from the grave" for future readers who fill out the contact form on your website.

YOUR BOOK FILES

To manage your estate, your heirs need access to your book files. Your book files are the crown jewels of your writing business—you must protect them at all costs. You must spare no expense to ensure that you and your heirs have access to all your book files at all times, no matter what.

Book files include:

- research
- original and edited manuscripts
- final formatted e-book, paperback, hardcover, large print, and audiobook files

- book covers and other design materials like promotional images
- licenses to use media such as the images and fonts on your book covers
- and more

If you don't take the time to organize your book project files and folders, then you're going to make things way too complicated for your heirs. If you have a lot of books like I do, organizing your books might prove to be impossible.

If you need some help getting organized, I wrote a book called **Keep Your Books Selling: Manage Your Book Portfolio to Make More Money** that will help you gather everything you need so that all your book project folders are organized logically and completely.

You'll need to organize your book files, but that is outside the scope of this book. What is in scope, however, is how your heirs will access your files.

Earlier in this book, I wrote that you need to make sure your heirs know the passwords and passcodes to your devices, including your writing computer.

Your heirs also need to know where your book files are located.

You must also take steps to ensure that your book files are backed up safely and securely. This is important while you're alive, but it's also important for your heirs to know that your work is backed up and where they can find the backups.

Backing up your work is essential. Things happen. Computers fail. Even if you don't think it could happen to you, you owe it to yourself and your work to protect it.

Anything can happen at any time, especially after your death:

- What if your executor is working on your computer and accidentally spills coffee on it?
- What if your home is burglarized and your computer is stolen?
- What if your home burns down?
- What if your hard drive simply fails?

If you only have one copy of all your book files, you're living dangerously. Losing your book files is catastrophic to a writing business. It's even more catastrophic to heirs who may not know about everything that was destroyed or why it was important.

The most popular methods for backing up your book data are:

1. External hard drives
2. Cloud-based backups
3. Automated cloud-based backups
4. Paper copies

I've used all of these methods, and all are essential in protecting your work. You cannot afford to skip any of them.

SEPARATION, DIVERSIFICATION, AND DUPLICATION

. . .

First, let's go over a few risk management basics. These are principles that insurance industry professionals use to help customers protect their property. Insurance is all about protecting people and property, so we can learn a thing or two from the insurance world.

Separation is the physical division of property. For example, if you have two hard drives that contain your work, it's a smart idea to separate them in different locations so that if one hard drive is damaged, the other will be safe. The best place to separate to is a bank safe deposit box. Store USB hard drives there for safekeeping and swap them out on a regular schedule.

Diversification is the act of spreading out an investment across many products to avoid trouble if one product does poorly. Stocks are a classic example of diversification—a stockbroker wants a portfolio of many stocks in case one plummets.

For authors, diversifying your backups means backing up using different methods. Save your manuscripts in multiple formats—EPUB, Word, rich text. Back up using different services—in the cloud, on your computer, on an external hard drive, and so on. Make it so that you can access your work in its purest form no matter what happens.

Duplication is backing your work up to multiple places in case one fails. It goes hand-in-hand with diversification.

We can use separation, diversification, and duplication to back up our work and reduce the chances of an event happening that destroys everything.

EXTERNAL HARD DRIVES

Don't rely on your computer to save you. Use an external hard drive. Store backups of your manuscript on it in case your computer fails. The doomsday scenarios are endless.

External hard drives can also fail, so it pays to own at least two. You can usually pick them up cheaply during the holidays.

On Mac operating systems, you can sync your hard drive with Mac's Time Machine, which will automatically back up your work without you having to do anything. There are Windows equivalents of Time Machine as well. The key is that you want your backups to happen without you having to do anything. They should happen in the background. If you can do that, then you're doing it right.

The best rule of thumb is to have one external hard drive connected to your computer at all times and another that is not, but that you connect to back up your work on a regular schedule, like once per month or quarter. This way, if your connected external hard drive dies, you won't lose everything —you'll only lose the files that were created after the last time you connected your backup drive. Not perfect, but better than losing everything.

There are also portable USB drives (known as flash drives or thumb drives) that are cheap and easy to transport. These drives fit in your pocket, in a drawer, in a cup holder in your car, in a backpack, and so on. Take advantage of their portability.

These types of drives are best paired with a safe deposit box. Buy a couple and swap them in and out. The best time to do this is whenever you finish or publish a new book.

There is also another form of portable USB drive that is particularly useful for estate planning: a USB security drive (not to be confused with a USB security key that we discussed in the Two-Factor Authentication chapter). A USB security drive is a larger flash drive that has physical buttons that you use to encode a passcode into the device. You have to enter the passcode before plugging in the device or it won't work. This way, everything on the drive is password-protected and secure. The drive will also erase everything on it if a passcode is entered incorrectly 10 times in a row. (Another reason to write that passcode down!)

There are a few downsides to USB security drives. First, they're still USB hard drives and are just as susceptible to failure as any other drive you own. Second, they're not designed for heavy use. These are NOT drives you want to carry with you every day. They belong in a drawer, fire-resistant safe, or bank safe deposit box. Third, you don't want to use this as your only backup in case they fail, which could defeat the purpose of using them in the first place, as they can be expensive. Fourth, they are battery-powered, which means you need to charge them. If the battery dies, you have to charge it in a USB port for a while until the battery is ready for use.

You can also purchase security external hard drives that work the same way as their flash drive equivalents, but I think that's a little too much firepower. If that's you, though, go for it.

CLOUD STORAGE SERVICES

The cloud is a great place to save your work, but it alone won't save you. I never recommend that authors use the cloud as a sole backup method.

The cloud likes to stay current. When you change a file on your computer, it changes in the cloud, and vice versa. So, if you make an accidental change and don't realize it for several days, you're screwed.

Also, file versioning in the cloud is lacking, since the cloud was never truly designed for this. Some services do offer versioning, but I wouldn't rely on them.

Cloud backups are part of a bigger strategy. They play a part, but they shouldn't be the only part.

AUTOMATED CLOUD-BASED BACKUPS: THE LAST LINE OF DEFENSE

And now we arrive at an underutilized backup method that works so well, it's (almost) foolproof. Yet few people know this method exists. I'm referring to automatic backup services such as Backblaze, Carbonite, and more. These programs automatically back up everything on your computer to the cloud, but the difference is that they make several backups per day and create an archive of your backups that you can access at any time from any computer with an Internet connection. The real advantage of these programs is that you can access them even if your computer is destroyed. Just find another computer, log in, and you can download the files you need. For an added charge, they'll even ship you a hard drive with your data on it.

Your backups are also secure, so that if someone hacks your computer, they can't access your backups without your username, password, and method of two-factor authentication. Your backups aren't going anywhere, and these companies guarantee it.

Not only will these services back up your computer, but they'll also back up any external hard drives connected to your computer. Goodbye hard drive failure! If your drive dies, buy a new one and download your files onto it in minutes.

This is why I believe that automatic backup services are critical and required. No other backup method will give you as much protection. If you use this method in conjunction with the other backup methods I detailed in this chapter, then you'll have an almost foolproof backup system. I use and recommend Backblaze.

If your heirs live in another state, province, or country, this is also an effective way for them to access your book files without having to return to your city to obtain them. You'll also save them time and expense because they would have had to back up your files anyway.

These services only have a few weaknesses. The first is that you have to pay annual subscriptions. I believe the money is worth it for the peace of mind. Second, they're only effective if you use them correctly. If you don't follow instructions, then you may not back up your work correctly.

Backblaze has only ever failed me once, and it was my fault. I can't recommend it enough. There are many alternatives to Backblaze too, so do your homework.

PAPER COPIES

. . .

I have to mention paper copies because they're often forgotten in this technological age. It's a smart idea to keep paper copies of all your books. I used to avoid doing this—for a long time, I resisted the urge to build a "vanity" bookshelf of all my books. I'm a humble guy—I publish a book and move on to the next one.

But when I thought about it, I put my lack of vanity aside for a moment and realized that keeping paper copies is a really smart way to back up your work. What if the above backup methods fail? It's unlikely, but anything is possible. You'll always be able to scan your book, pay someone (or an app) to digitize the text, and then you're back in the game.

Of course, one major reason to avoid paper copies is that if you lose them, you lose your copy. Also, they're susceptible to fire, water, and the passage of time. But a vanity shelf can be a good thing if you treat it as a backup method!

BRINGING IT ALL TOGETHER

. . .

Here is my process for backing up my data:

- I have one external hard drive that is connected to my computer at all times. This drive is backed up multiple times per day automatically.
- I have another external hard drive that I connect to my computer on a regular schedule—once per month, or whenever I publish a new book. I back up all my work on this drive, in case anything happens to my primary hard drive.
- At the same time that I back up to my second external hard drive, I also back my work up on a flash drive. Quarterly, I take this flash drive to my bank safe deposit box, where I swap it out with another flash drive.
- I use a preferred cloud service to keep all my work current and also to store my book files.
- I use an automated cloud backup service to back up the files on my computer, the files in the cloud, and the files on my connected

external hard drive. These backups run multiple times per day. These backups can only be accessed securely and they cannot be deleted even if my computer is destroyed.

- Every time I publish a new book, I automatically order it in paperback format, and I store that on my vanity shelf, just in case.

My methods are redundant. For example, I probably don't need to be so religious about my external hard drives since Backblaze backs those up. Eventually, I'll relax a little, but I'm very, very particular about backing up my work.

Your Homework

If you aren't backing up your work religiously, automatically, and diligently, then you're asking for trouble. It's only a matter of time before you lose your work. When it happens, it will come out of nowhere. Trust me on this. When you're alive, you might be able to correct the problem, but when you're dead, your heirs won't stand a chance.

Take the time to plan your backups properly. Come up with a method and stick with it. Be patient, and you'll be fine. It may take a few months to get into a rhythm, but you'll be glad you did.

If you have a backup strategy, take a moment to give it a thorough inspection. Don't let yourself get complacent.

ACTION ITEMS

- Make sure you are backing up your book files religiously, automatically, and diligently.
- Practice the art of separation, diversification, and duplication regularly.
- Inform your heirs where your book files are located and how to access the backups if something were to happen.

BANK ACCOUNTS

I lost two nights of sleep researching this chapter.

My research started with a simple question: "What happens to my bank accounts after I die?"

The answer wasn't simple, and it took me down a terrifying rabbit hole that, frankly, scared the hell out of me. My greatest hope is that this chapter will scare the hell out of you so that you'll take the necessary steps to protect your heirs.

Let's also get some very stern rules out of the way:

1. In every country I researched, it is **illegal** to withdraw money from a deceased

person's bank account unless it is court-approved. This applies to in-person and online transactions. If your heirs do this without the advisement of an attorney, they could face serious legal consequences.

2. Not even a person who has power of attorney over you can access your accounts once you die. (i.e., Your child had POA over you because you were dying from a terminal illness and was using your bank account daily. Now they can't.)

3. The moment your bank finds out you're dead, it will freeze your account. This will happen immediately and will last until the bank receives assurance from the state that it is okay to release the funds.

4. Once an account is frozen, the bank will not comply with any request to withdraw money—not even from an executor—unless it is court-approved. If money must be withdrawn for something like a funeral, the bank may insist that they pay the funeral home directly. This protection exists for the deceased and creditors who

may have a claim to the money in the account. There are ways around this, but if you don't plan for it, your heirs may not have access to the funds they need to settle your estate, not to mention immediate living or business expenses.

5. For your heirs to claim the money in your bank accounts, they have to know the accounts exist. In today's age, you can open digital bank accounts in minutes with a bank that may not even have a physical presence in your area, making bank account discovery much harder. You must keep good records.

See why this is a Silver Bullet of Doom?

The information in this chapter applies to both your personal and your business money.

BANKING BASICS

. . .

When you opened your bank account, you did it in one of two ways: you either opened an account with one or more people (called joint ownership), or you opened it in your name only (or the name of your business).

In the case of a joint ownership account, we'll assume it's between two people, such as you and your spouse. There are different types of joint ownership, but the most common is joint tenancy with rights of survivorship. In this arrangement, you and your spouse have equal rights to the bank account and own everything in the bank account equally. If one of you dies, then the other will own everything in the account.

Another arrangement is tenancy in common, which means that when you die, the assets in your bank account pass according to your will.

To the question of "What happens to a joint account when you die," the simple answer is that, if the account is a joint tenancy account with rights of survivorship, the surviving owner receives the money, and that money does not go through probate. The surviving owner can access the bank account and use it as they regularly would. If the person you jointly own the bank account with dies before you, and you don't have a will, then the account may go through probate if you didn't follow at least one of the potential options discussed later.

If it is a tenancy in common account, however, then your assets will be frozen and subject to probate because they will pass according to your will.

There are, of course, nuances with both joint ownership account types and your attorney can help you understand them. If you don't know which type your bank account is, ask your bank. Then follow-up with your attorney.

In the case of an account you opened under your name only (or in the name of your business), you are the sole person who can access the account. To the question of "What happens to your solely-owned account when you die," there are two possible answers if you did not take additional steps to secure your account:

- The bank will freeze the account until your

estate is settled.

- The funds will sit unfrozen but dormant until your executor can withdraw them safely (because they cannot withdraw a dead person's money, remember).

How do you secure a bank account to keep the money available to your heirs?

One option is to make your heir(s) a co-signer on your account, but that's unwise.

Another option you could consider is making your account "POD or "transfer on death" (TOD). When the owner of a POD or TOD account dies, the bank will release the money to the beneficiary you designate, and the funds will not go through probate. However, POD designations are so powerful that they override wills. If your will states that all your money will go to your spouse but you have your uncle listed as a POD beneficiary, the bank must give the money to your uncle, and there's nothing your spouse can do about it. This would also apply to an ex-spouse if you forgot to update your POD designation…

I've read stories of people whose POD designations did not line up with their wills, therefore weakening their estate plans. POD designations will ensure that your heirs get your money quickly, but they are quite heavy-handed.

Another option you have to ensure that your heirs have access to your bank account is to use the benefits of a revocable living trust. The mechanics of how to do this are far too advanced and must be explained by an attorney, so you'll need to talk to one to see how you can use a trust to get around a bank freezing your accounts. As a reminder, assets in a trust do not go through probate.

Finally, if your business is a corporation or an LLC, then you're playing by a different set of rules, and you need to make sure you consult with your attorney about how to handle your succession. You may be able to avoid your bank accounts getting frozen with some solid and quick legal advice. It will probably be easier than you think.

The bottom line is that whatever you do and however you do it, you will need an attorney's help getting around your bank's rules legally. A lot of this is going to depend on the laws in your area and your bank's internal rules and protocols.

But that's not all. Even if we take the proper steps to fix the issues I just described, the silver bullet still has us in its sights.

FUTURE INCOME

The money in your business bank account right now is the money that is in your business bank account **right now**.

In about 30 days, more money is going to be deposited and withdrawn. Thirty days after that, it's going to happen again. This will continue for as long as you have a legal right to make money from your copyrights, if your heirs manage your estate correctly. In my case, my heirs can earn from my books 70 years after my death.

The nature of a publishing business is fluid— money flows to you both regularly and irregularly, but you never know how much you will receive.

One of your books might suddenly drop off in sales, or you might see unexplained spikes with another book—sometimes at the same time. If you're an influencer and you do affiliate marketing, you never quite know when you'll be paid or how much. If you're traditionally-published, publisher royalty statements may be up and down income-wise. If you do licensing deals, you might have signed a licensing agreement that said that the rights buyer will pay you if they do something additional with your content, like a magazine reprinting an article several years after first publication.

My point is that money flows to your publishing business in many different-sized income streams at different times.

That's where the problems start. When you die and you are the sole owner of an account, your bank will close your account. If you have a joint owner account, the bank may change the bank account number.

Once either of those scenarios happens, those revenue streams will no longer have a place to go. The book retailers (or publishers) you do business with will no longer have a valid bank account on file, which will cause all sorts of problems, usually starting with a flurry of emails that something is wrong with your account.

You may be thinking, "My heirs will have my passwords. They can just switch the bank account information on file."

Maybe, but only if you've done the proper planning with an estate attorney and an accountant.

Your goal needs to be the smooth transition of current and future money to your heirs.

Remember that there are tax implications too. Income is flowing to you (the deceased) under either an individual status or a business entity. The moment that changes and money starts flowing to an heir, it will trigger more issues your heirs will need to deal with on the tax side.

For example, if your spouse doesn't want to (or can't) continue your publishing business and just wants to live off your residual writing income, that is a colossal tax change. Or, if your heirs set up a trust and begin operating it to carry out your estate endeavors, and they want your book income to flow into the trust, that's also a situation that requires a lawyer and an accountant. They're effectively taking over your publishing business.

I can't tell you what you should do. I raise the issue merely so you can become aware and start planning for your specific situation.

Be very, very careful when planning a smooth transition of your current and future money. Your heirs will depend on the income.

ACTION ITEMS

- Make an inventory of all bank accounts you own personally and in your business. Include the names on the account, account, routing, debit and credit cards, PINs, bank deposit boxes, whether you have designated POD, and anything else that will help your executor get a clear financial picture of your estate.
- Make an inventory of all the income

streams you have had, currently have, and anticipate having, and which bank account(s) each income stream flows into.

- Make an inventory of all the recurring expenses that are charged to your bank account, credit, or debit cards. Note whether each can be kept or canceled after your death.

- Find out how your bank(s) handles the death of a customer and note any differences for your executor.

- Discuss with your estate attorney the best way to avoid an asset freeze to keep your current bank assets available to your heirs.

- Discuss with your estate attorney the safest legal way to reroute the flow of future money; discuss when it can start and how to do it without making mistakes. Instructions will need to be communicated very clearly to your heirs.

- Discuss the tax ramifications of your strategy with your accountant.

TAXES

No matter what your estate planning arrangements are, your heirs probably won't inherit your estate tax-free. There are a few obligations you need to keep in mind during your planning.

The names of taxes are different internationally, so do local research to determine what you might owe after death. This chapter is a general overview.

INCOME TAX

. . .

You still owe income and/or self-employment tax on all income you earned while you were alive during the tax year in which you die. If you die on June 1st, you'll owe taxes up to that point.

If you owe back taxes, your estate will have to pay those too, so don't avoid your taxes while you're alive!

Your executor will need to file a tax return on your behalf. This means that you will need to keep clean and organized expense and income records at all times. If you live in the United States, it is recommended that you keep at least your last three years of tax returns in case of an audit. (Honestly, you should keep all your tax returns, and that's good practice no matter where you live.)

Your executor needs to know where your tax records are as well as password information for online bookkeeping software you might use, like QuickBooks or Xero. They also need the name and contact information of your accountant. Assuming you hired a good accountant, if your heirs can use that person, that's preferable, since they will be familiar with you and your business.

If you leave a mess for your executor at tax time, it could drain money from your estate. I once hired a terrible accountant who insisted that I owed thousands in taxes, only to discover that they missed critical deductions (because I wasn't organized **and** because the accountant wasn't skilled).

No one knows your business better than you. Don't set your executor up for failure.

ESTATE INCOME TAX

Any income that your estate generates after your death and until the estate is settled is also taxable. The name for this tax varies by country, but it is not paid by your heirs—it is paid from your estate.

This applies not only to real estate and investments but also your copyrights. After you're dead, book income will continue to pour into your bank accounts. You'll owe taxes on that income until your estate is settled. That's why it's a good idea to talk to an estate lawyer, a tax lawyer, and an accountant to develop a strategy of how, when, and where to transition your book income so you can minimize this.

However, the moment your heirs reroute the money, **your** income becomes **their** income, so there are tax consequences no matter what you do.

ESTATE TAX

An estate tax (also known as a death tax) is a one-time tax on your estate. It is due in addition to any other taxes you may owe.

In the United States, there are two possible estate taxes: federal and state. At the time of this writing, the federal exemption is up to 12.06 million dollars, meaning you will not pay an estate tax unless your estate exceeds that amount. State estate tax thresholds vary, and not every state has an estate tax.

Be careful with estate taxes because this is one area where the Silver Bullet of Doom can hit your estate.

Here's a riddle. You're a full-time author making $100,000 per year. In planning your financial future, you meet with your financial adviser, who asks you to inventory all your assets. You estimate that your family would need at least $750,000 to settle any debts after your death—mortgages, student loans, credit card debt, and so on. You buy life insurance based on that number.

You die suddenly. During probate, it is determined that the value of your estate isn't $750,000, **but $7.5 million.**

What happened?

Your copyrights are what happened. You forgot to account for the fact that your copyrights are assets that have value too. Don't forget about this in your estate planning.

If you're making $100,000 from your books at the time of your death, then a court could reasonably assume that you could make that for at least 70 years after your death, maybe more. If one of your books takes off or is adapted into a movie, the value of your IP could be even higher.

You should also know that, in most places, your attorney and your executor are entitled to a percentage of your estate, so undervaluing your estate has bigger consequences.

If such a scenario were to happen, it could bankrupt your heirs because if your estate can't pay for the taxes and legal fees…then your heirs will have to. And if your heirs file for bankruptcy, a court will seize your copyrights and sell them off for pennies on the dollar, ending your author estate.

There's that silver bullet…

Could such a scenario happen? Yes, it's possible, but hopefully, it will be unlikely for a few reasons.

- There are many different ways to value IP. There is no commonly-accepted method, and some methods produce higher values than others. This is a complex area of the law.

- As we discussed in the Last Will chapter, if you use your will correctly to assign your copyrights to your spouse or a trust (or another person permitted in your area per local probate law), then your copyrights won't go through probate. You may still have to value them, but the value should hopefully be exempt from taxation.
- There are many other factors a court will consider in valuing your IP. A poetry collection might not be worth as much as a bestselling science fiction novel. If you have one book, that's different than if you have three hundred.

So, while your estate probably won't receive a tax bill that is millions higher than expected, it is a safe bet to assume that your intellectual property **will** increase the value of your estate, and you should keep that in mind when planning for the future.

How much is your copyright worth? That's a question no one can answer, not even most attorneys, which makes IP valuation maddening. You can get your IP professionally valued, but unless you are making a lot of money, it may not be practical. Just know that it is an option down the road for you (or your heirs).

INHERITANCE TAX

An inheritance tax is a one-time tax on assets received from a deceased person. An inheritance tax is paid by your heirs.

Depending on where you live, inheritance taxes can be non-existent, modest, or substantial. I live in the state of Iowa, and Iowa just repealed inheritance taxes as long as you pass property down to a spouse or children. (Yay Iowa!) My heirs will not pay an inheritance tax after my passing.

Nebraska, the state to my west, has an inheritance tax of up to 18 percent.

Missouri, the state to my south, has no inheritance tax at all.

A few hours' drive makes all the difference in the world, but a plane trip halfway across the world shows how inheritance taxes can really vary!

My friends down under in Australia don't have inheritance taxes. South Africans also enjoy no inheritance taxes.

My friends across the pond in England, however, could pay an inheritance tax as high as 40 percent!

Talk about stark contrasts.

You'll need to research inheritance taxes for your area and ways to reduce them if you think your heirs will owe them.

And remember, just because your heirs don't owe an inheritance tax doesn't mean they won't have to pay taxes of some kind!

ACTION ITEMS

- Determine which estate and inheritance taxes apply to you and your heirs.
- Get your tax paperwork in order. Make

plans to pay back taxes if you owe them. Don't die with a tax mess for your executor to clean up.

- Meet with your estate planning attorney and your accountant to plan your estate. Plan early, often, and regularly.

YOUR DOMAINS AND YOUR WEBSITES

Your website is a critical part of your author business ecosystem, and it will be even more important after your death.

Your website is your home base. It's where readers can learn about you, your books, and where to buy them.

When I first entered publishing in 2012, websites were important, but there were a lot of authors who couldn't be bothered with setting one up. Influencers urged how critical they were, but it wasn't uncommon to meet authors who didn't have websites.

Today, most self-respecting authors wouldn't be caught dead without one. Everyone understands now that the authors who didn't have websites got left behind.

Given this truth, it's unfortunate that more authors don't take steps to safeguard their domains. The first indicator of a dead author is a lapsed domain. I've seen it more times than I like to count.

If you don't have a website, then readers can't find you. If they can't find you, then they can't buy your books. If they can't buy your books, then your heirs will lose out on income.

Your heirs don't have to actively update your website. After all, you'll be dead, so there may not be much "new" content, if any. But they should keep your domain bills paid and your website operational. Every once in a while, they should hire someone to update the design and the content.

I believe it's best to think about your website and domain like a piece of real estate. Just like you'd maintain a home to pass down to your heirs, you also want to make investments and updates to your website so that it grows in value over time. If you and your heirs do it right, your website might see far more traffic after your death than you ever saw while you were alive.

DOMAIN BASICS

Simply put, a domain is the name of a website. One of my domains is authorlevelup.com. You have to choose a domain that no one else is using, and you must pay an annual fee to keep it. If you don't, the name will lapse and someone else can buy it.

Domains are incredibly valuable. Some of the most popular websites on the Internet are domain names that were purchased in the '90s when few truly understood how valuable they would be. Think aa.com for American Airlines or Cars.com.

Domains are so valuable that companies will pay big money to acquire a domain name from an existing owner. At the time of this writing, the most expensive   domain   ever   purchased   is carinsurance.com, for which the current owner paid $872 million!

If you own the rights to a domain right now but it lapses after you die, someone will almost certainly buy it. And, as is the case with many lapsed domains that get acquired, the owner may do nothing with it. If your heirs want it back, they will have to contact the owner of the domain and pay for it. Chances are, they'll have to pay a lot of money, probably more than they can afford.

As a result, an innocent oversight on your part will damage your author legacy because:

- all the links in the back of your books will now be invalid.
- you will lose all the data on your website too.
- any website or social media post that is linked to your website will now be invalid, and there will be nothing your heirs can do about it.
- your heirs will have to purchase a new website.

- losing a domain will be a massive headache.

The term domain is also loosely used to describe the entire property that your website rests on. When you purchase a domain, you also purchase a website hosting package and the rights to access a backend dashboard to create and administer your website. When I use the term domain from now on, I'm referring to both your domain name and your website.

When you purchase the rights to a domain name, you register it with a website hosting provider. These providers include Bluehost, GoDaddy, HostGator, DreamHost, and Namecheap, to name a few. Your hosting plan includes the ability to install content management software such as WordPress. It also includes domain-specific email addresses that you can use for branding purposes.

Website hosting plans cost more than domain names, but they're still relatively inexpensive. I pay around $300 per year for my plan. When you add in domains, I pay around $350 per year for the right to operate my websites. I think of it as rent, and that's pretty cheap rent.

HOW DOMAINS DIE

I can only speculate why author domains have lapsed over the years, but I have some theories.

The most obvious explanation is the author wasn't prudent enough to leave a list of their online accounts. And (Or), they didn't leave the passwords to those accounts, so the heirs couldn't manage the domain. When the heirs shut down the author's credit card, the domain lapsed.

Another explanation is that an heir saw a charge on the deceased author's credit card statement, thought it was fraudulent, and requested a chargeback, triggering the hosting provider to cancel the account. Maybe the heir realized their mistake after the fact, maybe not.

Or, the heirs canceled the domain without understanding (or caring about) the consequences.

Or, the heirs realized they could save a few hundred dollars and so they closed the account out of necessity.

The final explanation is that the heirs just didn't want to deal with the burden of managing a domain.

Whatever the explanation, the root cause is almost always a lack of understanding of how important domains are. Any and all blame for a mistake this colossal only rests with the author, not the heirs.

If you want to have a literary estate, your heirs must understand the importance of maintaining an operational, up-to-date, well-designed website with little to no bugs. Otherwise, it's to their detriment. You'll be dead, so it won't matter to you if they screw this up, but they need to know that if they cut off a domain, they're cutting off income and making their lives infinitely more difficult.

When you're planning your estate, your domain requires special care. You have two goals:

1. To ensure that the domain does not lapse under any circumstances.
2. To ensure that your heirs successfully assert control over the domain.

The key question we must address is what happens to the ownership of your hosting account when you die. If we address that, we can achieve both goals.

CHANGING OWNERSHIP OF YOUR HOSTING ACCOUNT: THE SIMPLE PATH

When you open a hosting account, it's in your name, but with many providers, you can change the name on the account at any time.

Unless the terms of service forbid it, your heirs may be able to log in, change the name on the account to theirs, and update the credit card on file. If they can do that, then that is the answer to this silver bullet. (But they shouldn't do anything with your account until cleared by your estate attorney.)

Another thing to understand is that large companies set their domains up to have perpetual ownership. In fact, I checked the domain name for my employer, and they don't even have a person listed as an owner. The company is listed as the owner, and a certain job position is listed as the contact information. Even if the person who works that position changes, it doesn't matter. It seems that domain providers do not care very much about the account owner so long as the domain is paid for and there are no terms of service violations—but that's Michael La Ronn's opinion only. Just something to think about.

CHANGING OWNERSHIP OF YOUR HOSTING ACCOUNT: THE NOT-SO-SIMPLE PATH

If the terms of service don't allow for a simple name change, then your heirs will need to notify the hosting provider and follow the company's protocols for them to acknowledge your heirs and transfer the account to their name.

Search for terms like "deceased" and "death of a customer" to find these rules. I reviewed the websites of five major hosting providers in researching this book, and all of them had pages that clearly outlined the company's rules for transfers. As long as your heirs follow the rules exactly, they should be fine.

If your heirs go this route, they should expect to produce a lot of paperwork and anticipate a lot of questions. While it may be unlikely, the hosting provider can refuse a transfer request.

Also, if this is the path your heirs must go down, be empathetic to the fact that they may not know anything about domains, and it may be intimidating for them. Include links to pages that contain rules they need to follow, and also include customer support phone numbers and emails in case they run into trouble.

ACTION ITEMS

- Communicate the importance of maintaining your website to your heirs.
- Inventory all domains you have.
- Research your hosting provider's terms for changing the ownership on your account. If your heirs can simply change the name on the account with no adverse consequences, they should do that.
- If the hosting provider requires notice of your death, find the page on their website that contains transfer protocols. Share that with your heirs to save them from having to dig around.

YOUR ACCOUNTS WITH BOOK RETAILERS

When you publish a book (independently), you publish on Amazon, Barnes & Noble, Kobo, Apple, Google Play, and more. You may also publish with book aggregators like Draft2Digital, Smashwords, and PublishDrive. You need to know what happens to your accounts after your death.

Nothing in this chapter should be taken as legal advice. This is a difficult topic that ultimately requires the guidance of your estate lawyer. When you die, your royalties become part of your estate, which means they could be subject to probate. Also, retailers change their terms of service and guidelines all the time, so don't rely solely on this book to do your planning. Use this information as a starting point for your own research, and no matter what you do, instruct your heirs to always talk to a lawyer before they do anything with your accounts, especially updating names or bank information. You don't want your heirs to run afoul of retailers' terms of service and/or probate laws in your country, especially if they change something before they're legally entitled to do so.

Let me summarize my findings about book retailers, and then I'll get into the details.

- You MUST preserve your account usernames, passwords, and two-factor authentication for your heirs, or you will make this way more difficult than it needs to be.
- The more accounts you have, the more complex your situation will be.
- Terms of service are everything in this struggle. It's up to you and your heirs to monitor retailer terms of service and make sure that you do not violate them. Retailers update their terms and guidelines often.

- The clearest, simplest path of least resistance may be for your heirs to continue using your various accounts until they are forced to do otherwise. If a retailer offers the ability to add an heir as a user to your account, you should strongly consider doing so while you are alive.
- Your heirs should always be prepared to provide a death certificate, will, and legal documents proving their ownership of the copyrights if required by the retailer.
- Did I mention that you should talk to a lawyer about this?

SOME QUICK WORDS IN RETAILERS' DEFENSE

Retailers are in the business of selling books.

When you open an account, you're the only person who uses it. The retailer knows that you will be the only person they have to contend with. If you're a pain in the ass or if you violate the terms of service, they can cancel your account.

When you die, your copyrights will be transferred to your heirs. I would imagine that most authors would have more than one heir by law. (If you have a spouse and at least one child, that's two. Siblings and living parents can also be heirs.)

Now the retailers suddenly have multiple people they have to deal with, all of whom have a claim to your book sales. And as we know, heirs don't always get along. Sometimes they go to court.

As I said, retailers are in the business of selling books. They are not in the business of settling estate disputes.

What happens if Heir A presents a copy of the death certificate and legal documents to a retailer, the retailer switches the account to their name, and then Heir B arrives with the death certificate and the *real* legal documents?

What happens if your executor gets the account transferred to their name, flees the country, and leaves the rest of your heirs penniless?

What happens if Retailer A releases your account to Heir A, but Retailer B has lax internal protocols and accidentally releases the account to Heir B, who was not supposed to have it?

You can see where I'm going with this. Retailers don't want to get sued, and I don't blame them.

But this aversion to lawsuits is probably one reason why there isn't much information publicly on their websites about how they handle situations where the author has died.

So, I embarked on a quest to see if I could find the answers for myself: by reviewing retailers' terms of service and contacting them directly to see what information they would share with me. What I really wanted was some assurance that they have internal guidelines and that they would recognize my heirs. If possible, I wanted to find out any unusual nuances for each retailer so I could plan for them.

There are several questions we need to answer, and the answer will differ for each retailer:

- What happens to your account when you die?
- Does the retailer have an inactivity policy that could trigger the deletion of your account, and if so, how can your heirs avoid that policy?
- Can your heirs continue using your account or do they need to create a new account?
- If they must create a new account, can your books, metadata, sales data, and reviews be transferred, or do your heirs have to start from scratch?

Also, there's another thing I want to address before we dig into the details. Many retailers contain language in their terms that says that you are responsible for your account and that you may not permit a third party to access your account. Some authors I have talked to have expressed concern that this means that your heirs cannot access your account without violating the terms of service.

Legally, I don't know if that is true or not, but I do know two things for sure:

- If you read the terms of service for most retailers, the terms are binding not only to you, but also to your heirs and successors. One could interpret this to mean that retailers permit your heirs to use your accounts after your death.

- Without exception, all the retailer customer service representatives I spoke with advised me that it is okay for heirs to log in to your account after you pass away under the condition that they have the legal right to do so. In fact, at some retailers, the only way to continue your author operations after your death is for your heirs to use your existing account. I take anything a customer service representative gives me with a grain of salt (and you should too), but at least retailers gave me *something* to work with.

AMAZON

. . .

There are a few things about Amazon that I should point out that make estate planning with them a potential headache if you use more than one of their services.

First, you can only have one Amazon account. That account allows you to sign up for any of Amazon's optional services. For example, I have an Amazon store account where I order things. When I signed up for KDP, I did it with my Amazon store account username and password. Same with ACX, Amazon Associates, Amazon Ads, and other services I use for the company.

If you delete your Amazon account, you are technically deleting everything, including your KDP account.

Here's what their website says about closing your account: "Note: Once your account has been closed, all of the products and services accessed through your account will no longer be available to you, across any Amazon sites globally."

I spoke with an Amazon representative who confirmed that anything you do with your Amazon account will have downstream consequences to other Amazon services you use.

Make sure your heirs do not delete your master Amazon store account! They might be tempted to do it while wrapping up your estate; this is not immediately intuitive if you don't use Amazon's ecosystem every day.

Another curious thing about your Amazon account is that, if you read the Amazon store terms of service, there is nothing in the terms about requiring a legal name for an account. If I wanted, I could change the name on the account at any time —I could use my real name, my initials, my pen name, or a screen name like ringydingding123. The name on the Amazon account is the public name, but at the end of the day, they'll still need my real name when I give my credit card or when I attach a bank account.

My first thought was, "Why can't my wife just log in and change the name on the account to hers?" This way, it would preserve any connections my existing account has to Amazon's subsidiary services.

But I don't know if you can do that. When I asked the question, "If I were to pass away, could my wife change the name on my account to hers and continue using it?" to a customer service representative using Amazon's chat feature, they said yes, she could. Some context clues made me question if I was talking to a live person, so I called them and got an actual live person on the phone. The second representative told me that my wife needed to open a new account and that she could not continue using my account. Data cannot be transferred between Amazon accounts.

Ugh…

That said, I don't know if Amazon intends for customer accounts to persist indefinitely, or if they will ever purge accounts at some point. They're still a relatively young company. It's impossible to know for sure what actions they will take, say, 50 years from now.

If there's one thing I know from working in corporate America for a long time, it's that companies make decisions based on dollars and cents. Having a bunch of inactive users costs money, especially if they've been deceased for a long time and there's no activity on the account.

Why do I care about inactivity?

There's the possibility that your heirs might not want to run a publishing business at the level you do currently. They might just want a direct deposit every month. They may only log in to a retailer if there's a problem with the account. In any case, it's probably safe to say that they won't log in to your Amazon or other retailer accounts nearly as much as you do. And if your heir's heir passes away, who knows how active they might be? All these possibilities make your heirs targets for inactivity policies, and it's not uncommon for digital companies to clean house every once in a while. I share this mainly as a cautionary tip for your heirs to be aware of.

As far as your Amazon master account goes, there's a 50-50 chance that your heirs can use an existing account or will be forced to create a new one. It all boils down to the company's terms of service and their internal rules and protocols at the time of your death, which could be drastically different than what is presented in this chapter.

AMAZON KDP

Amazon master account findings aside, remember that every service you use at Amazon is either a different department or a different company altogether.

For years, KDP authors have been in the dark about what happens when an author dies. I've searched in previous years, but I never saw anything on their website that indicated their position. Fortunately, when I was writing this book, KDP updated their "Manage Your Account" page to include instructions about managing a deceased author's account. It was added on November 23, 2021, after over a decade of no answers.

Here's what it says as of December 30, 2021:

. . .

"Our team can help you during this difficult time. To request access to a KDP author's account after they have passed away or become incapacitated, please contact us. To access the contact us form, either sign-in or create a free KDP account. We take security very seriously, so before we can help you access the account, you will need to provide the following documentation:

Death certificate

One of the following court-issued letters indicating that you own the rights to the account:

Estate Owner

Next Executor

Next of kin

Will

Once you have access to the account, our team can help you to either close, merge, or take ownership of the account."

·   ·   ·

Also on this page is a section titled "Merge Accounts." Here's what it says:

"To have your accounts merged, you need to contact us. You will need to:

- Ensure to write from the email address associated with [the] KDP account you want to merge to another account.
- Provide a title of one book from each KDP account and its corresponding ASIN or ISBN.
- Have live titles in both account[s].
- Remove any Ads promoting your KDP titles and create new Ads from your new account.
- Ensure your account information is updated to pay any outstanding royalties. Learn more about updating bank details.

Note: We cannot move specific titles/draft titles from one account to another.

Merging your KDP accounts will move your published books from your old KDP account to your new one. The below information will not be transferred:

- Old account information
- Tax interview details
- Sales reports
- Payment information to the new account
- Active Ads running for your title published in [the] old account
- A+ Content. You can replicate your projects on the new account.

Reports will no longer be accessible with the old account. We recommend downloading your reports before merging accounts.

After you gather the information we need and verify your account details, contact us. We'll move the old account and then confirm that this is done."

In short, your heir can take ownership of the account or, if they happen to be an author, they can get the books transferred to their KDP account.

Depending on when you read this, please look up the page yourself to confirm if the language is the same or if it has changed. Also, make sure to verify the rules for your specific country, as they could be different. But man, that is a relief. At least I know there are options for preserving my *books*.

(As a side note, remember that even if KDP allows a new owner or merges accounts, there could still be disputes between your heirs.)

In doing some additional research, I found a blog post by an author whose mother (also an author) passed away and transferred the copyrights via a will. The author wrote that Amazon accepted a copy of a will, death certificate, and legal documents without any questions and were very helpful in guiding her through the process of transferring the books from her mother's KDP account to hers. The links to the books remained the same, and I presume no reviews were lost either. She didn't say it explicitly, but it appears that she followed KDP's merging guidelines. So, there is at least a record of one person who successfully transferred their rights after death, which is encouraging.

As clear as the KDP guidelines are, there *is* a silver bullet hidden in the merging option, and I hope you saw it. If not, here it is:

"The below information will not be transferred: Active Ads running for your title published in [the] old account."

AMAZON ADS

If your heirs merge your KDP with theirs, they will lose existing ads.

If Amazon Ads are a significant contributor to your income, losing your ads is a problem.

I reviewed the Amazon Advertising website to see if they had similar deceased/merging guidelines. I didn't find anything, so I called them.

The representative was very friendly and helpful and she told me that they do not operate like KDP.

There is no way to transfer existing ads on your account to the account of another person. This means that your heirs will have to start from scratch and recreate any ads that you had running. Naturally, that's troublesome because there's no guarantee that the new ads will perform as effectively as the old ones.

Just to be sure, I followed up with an email, playing dumb to see if I would get a different answer. I did not, and the representative confirmed that you cannot transfer ads from one account to another.

So, this is what will happen if you transfer accounts:

- Your heirs will contact KDP to inform them of your death and merge accounts.
- KDP will merge the accounts, cutting off your ads.
- Your heirs will have to create ads from scratch or hire an ad agency to assist.

Based on this information, if Amazon Ads are money makers for you, you *definitely* want your heirs to take over ownership of your KDP account so they don't lose existing ads. But if they do that, they're still subject to anything that can happen to your Amazon master account. As we discussed, it's unclear what Amazon could do to your master account and what their philosophy is. No matter what you do, there are risks.

AUDIBLE CREATION EXCHANGE (ACX)

There's also the Audible Creation Exchange (ACX), where authors create and publish audiobooks.

The ACX terms and website are silent about deceased authors, so I called them to ask what provisions they have in place and whether they allow account merging. ACX is particularly problematic because of royalty shares, which are indefinite between an author and narrator.

The ACX representative told me that they do have the ability to transfer books between accounts, but she advised that the heir could also log in and change the contact information to their name, as well as the bank and tax information. Any existing contracts with narrators (such as royalty shares) would continue until the author's heir or narrator canceled them.

AMAZON ASSOCIATES

Because I'm a glutton for punishment, I also chatted with Amazon Associates because I make money from them too. Amazon Associates is structured a little differently; the representative told me that I could add my heir as a Reports Access user (formerly known as a secondary user) on the account, and then when I die, the heir can log in and change themselves to a Full Access user (formerly known as a primary user). The representative confirmed that there is no way to transfer affiliate tags to another person's account.

To see what other options might be available, I spoke with the team at Genius Link, which is a link aggregation service that geolocates Amazon (and other) retailer affiliate links so that you can redirect users to the Amazon store in their country as well as do other sophisticated things. They advised that their service lets you update your Amazon Associates tag codes in your Genius Link account so that all of your affiliate links are updated at the source. So, if your heir needed to create another Amazon Associates account, they could use your existing Genius Link account to change all of your existing affiliate links in just a few minutes. A service like Genius Link could be helpful to your heirs in this regard.

Anyway, that's Amazon. I hope you can see the contradictions in terms of how each department handles the succession of accounts.

Is your brain fried yet? I hate to tell you this, but we're just getting started!

APPLE BOOKS

. . .

(If you don't publish your books to Apple directly but use an aggregator service like Draft2Digital, skip the rest of this section.)

Apple is similar to Amazon in that you have one Apple ID that gets you into all of Apple's services. Your Apple ID is your master key.

Your first step is to secure your Apple ID with a strong password and two-factor authentication.

There is a potential silver bullet you need to be careful of with Apple: Legacy Contacts. In 2021, Apple released a new feature called Legacy Contacts that allows you to designate someone to receive your Apple data after you die.

(But they don't get all of your Apple data; there's fine print you need to read.)

If you designate a Legacy Contact, the moment your heir reports your death to Apple, your Apple ID will be deactivated, and your Apple ID and password will no longer work on any of Apple's services. Your account will then be deleted in three years, and, if my understanding is correct, so will your iTunes Connect account because it requires your Apple ID.

As with everything in this chapter, read the fine print for yourself to make sure it's still accurate depending on when you read this book. Many are touting the Legacy Contacts feature as a must-use, but this is another example where an innocent mistake on your part could harm your book sales. Be careful.

And we haven't even discussed Apple Books yet!

If you publish books directly to Apple, at the time of this writing, your account is governed by the iTunes Connect terms of service. At some point, I anticipate Apple will change the name of the service because iTunes has been replaced with Apple Music.

The Apple representative I spoke with recommended adding additional Administrator and Legal users to your account in iTunes Connect. This way, there is always an authorized user on the account who can update the account or banking details.

When you add an authorized user to the account, that person has to enter their own unique Apple ID to sign up, so even if your account is deleted, that person will still be able to access and use iTunes Connect. An Apple representative confirmed that as long as the user is an Administrator and/or Legal User, your account may be deleted, but any Administrative and Legal users you've added can continue using the account and managing your books under their Apple IDs.

Apple does not have a specific inactivity policy, but users will need to agree to updated terms of service and banking information from time to time, and if that is not done, then your heirs will be unable to update your books.

AUTHOR'S REPUBLIC

Author's Republic is a popular audiobook distributor. The representative I spoke with advised that the only way for your heirs to continue earning sales commissions on your account is to access your existing Author's Republic account (and your PayPal account, where they deposit the money).

The representative confirmed that as long as they have your login details, they can log in and update the name on the account to their name as well as the banking information.

BARNES & NOBLE (BARNES & NOBLE PRESS)

The representative I spoke with suggested contacting the Barnes & Noble Press support team and advised that your heirs would need to provide a copy of a death certificate and legal documents verifying executor/heir status. They do not have an inactivity policy.

DRAFT2DIGITAL

. . .

The representative said that your heirs need to reach out to Draft2Digital's support team and they can help your heir take ownership of the account. The account will pass to your executor.

Additionally, Draft2Digital offers a Paid Collaborator feature that allows coauthors to share royalties with minimal effort. Existing Paid Collaborator agreements will remain in place. If the surviving coauthor and heirs decide to do something different, they can amend the agreement, but Draft2Digital will not be involved with this. I discuss coauthoring later in the book.

And finally, don't forget that if you use Draft2Digital, you also have a Books2Read account, which is a link aggregation service and a helpful marketing tool. I confirmed that all of your existing universal book links will remain intact.

Kudos to Draft2Digital for having plans in place and making it easy for author heirs!

Also, Draft2Digital acquired Smashwords in 2022, so these guidelines will eventually apply to Smashwords. Before the acquisition, Smashwords required a copy of the author's will and proof of executorship, so there were no major changes in this area as part of the acquisition.

FINDAWAY VOICES

Findaway Voices is another audiobook distributor.

The representative I spoke with recommended leaving login credentials to your heir. They can update the name and bank information on the account.

INGRAMSPARK

The representative I spoke with recommended adding your heir as a user to the account. When an author or publisher passes away and the heirs contact IngramSpark, they immediately escalate the request and will ask for more information from the executor of the estate. If the heir has account access, then they may be able to bypass some of this because adding a user to your account gives Ingram permission to speak with them regarding your account.

The representative didn't say it, but I got the sense that Ingram probably wants a heads-up that you've died.

Additionally, I found some account transfer guidelines on IngramSpark's website. They allow you to transfer files and information from one Lightning Source or IngramSpark account to another. The details are in the User Guide on their website, and as with anything in this chapter, they are always subject to change.

GOOGLE PLAY

(As a reminder, if you don't publish your books to Google directly but use an aggregator service, skip this section.)

Google is similar to Amazon and Apple in that your Google account is your master key. It gets you into all of Google's services like Gmail, YouTube, and Google Play. If you delete your Google account, you delete everything.

Google also is the most vigilant about inactive accounts, and one of the reasons why I'm extra cautious about inactivity.

As we discussed in the Email chapter, your Gmail account has an Inactivity policy: "Use the product to remain active. Activity includes accessing the product or its content at least every [two] years. We may take action on inactive accounts, which may include deleting your messages from the product." Additionally, another clause states, "If you're over your [storage] quota for [two] years or longer... [and] if you don't free up or purchase more space to get back under quota, all of your content may be removed from [Google]."

If you use Gmail and your heirs combine your inbox with theirs, use forwarding, keep your email storage under Google's quota, and log in to the Google Play Partner Center regularly, then I believe that would count as "activity." Hopefully, that would fly under Google's radar, but I don't know for sure.

If Google is not part of the services you or your heirs will use as part of your author estate, then they may be targeted by Google's inactivity detection. I share that so you know what could be working against your heirs.

The Google Play Partner Center works similarly to Apple Books in that you can add users to your account and give them different permission levels. Any users you add must sign in with their Google accounts.

I contacted Google Play's support team and asked them specifically if an author's Google account were to be deleted, would any users added to the Google Play Partner Center Account be able to access and manage books in the author's Google Play dashboard. They advised that as long as you add your heir to your Google Play Partner Center Account as an administrator, the deletion of your Google account will not affect the existence of the Partner Center account. Because your heirs must sign up as a user with their Google accounts, they will continue to be able to access and manage your books as if the account were theirs to begin with.

(By the way, I have to give Google Play a huge bravo because their customer service sent me an amazingly detailed email explaining exactly how this process works. Clearly, Google Play has thought about this. Their guidance was above and beyond anything else I received.)

KOBO

(This section only applies if you publish directly with Kobo.)

Kobo advised that if you have a publishing company listed on your account, then they will respect the transfer of your copyright as long as your successor provides proof. However, if you don't have a publishing company, then your heir will have to create a new account, delist the books from your current account, and then reupload them to the new one.

PAYHIP

Payhip is a direct sales retailer. They advised that if the heir has access to the account, they can continue using it and update it accordingly. They do not have an inactivity policy.

STREETLIB

They recommended that the heir contact their support team so they can help. They advised that if the heir has access to the account, they can continue using it and update it accordingly.

They do not have an inactivity policy.

FINAL THOUGHTS

. . .

There you go. If you ever wanted to know what will happen to your book retailer accounts after you die but were too shy to ask, now you know.

Let me say it again: nothing in this chapter is legal advice. Retailers change their terms of service and guidelines all the time, so don't rely on this book to do your planning. Use this information as a starting point, and no matter what you do, tell your heirs to always talk to a lawyer before they do anything with an account. You don't want to run afoul of probate laws in your country, especially if you change banking information before you're legally able to do so.

Here's a final thought. You might want to discuss this chapter with your heirs. Are they aware of how many dashboards they will have to access to manage your books? If I were an heir who knew nothing about publishing, this chapter would give me anxiety.

A potential helpful suggestion for your heirs could be consolidating your dashboards using an e-book aggregator like Draft2Digital, PublishDrive, or StreetLib. Use those to distribute your books everywhere except Amazon. I would leave your Amazon account alone, but it might be more empowering and comforting to your heirs if they only had to access two dashboards instead of ten.

I wouldn't rush off to consolidate your dashboards if you have no reason to do so, especially if it's disruptive to your sales or reviews, but maybe leave it as an option to your heirs and tell them how they can accomplish it. Or, if you know you're going to pass away, you could do it for them as one of your final acts.

ACTION ITEMS

- Preserve your account usernames, passwords, and two-factor authentication for your heirs.
- Review book retailers' terms of service and website details very carefully, and if necessary, contact their customer support team to learn how they treat deceased

authors' accounts and what steps your heirs will need to take to secure your books.

- Inform your heirs that they must speak with a lawyer before taking any action on any accounts to avoid issues with probate.
- Have a conversation with your heirs about just how many accounts they will need to manage and if they are comfortable with that. While you're alive, work together to develop a plan that will make account management less burdensome for them when you're gone.

SCAMS

Scammers are another Silver Bullet of Doom to prepare for.

Authors are magnets for scams. The same will be true for their heirs.

Think about it: an heir who has just inherited a portfolio of copyrights and who is contending with everything we've been discussing in this book is going to be massively overwhelmed. Massively overwhelmed is an understatement, actually.

Here's how it happens: your heir is going to be having a really bad day, maybe a low point. A smooth operator will contact them and promise to help them out...and because your heir is overwhelmed, you know the rest.

Scams that can befall your heirs include:

- spending an inordinate amount of money on services that provide little to no benefit
- stolen copyrights
- signing bad contracts that restrict what they can do with the copyrights
- disenfranchisement from the estate (i.e., a scammer steals the entire estate)
- and more

I recommend that you warn your heirs about scammers and things to be on the lookout for. My prediction is that heirs will fall for the same scams that authors fall for.

Authors are notorious for giving their power away. They're so busy being artists that they don't want to deal with the business and marketing parts of running a writing business. As a result, they're prone to waving their hands and giving those responsibilities over to other people.

Examples of people authors give their power to:

- traditional publishers
- literary agents
- editors
- publicists
- assistants

I'm not saying all publishers, agents, and so on are scammers. I am saying that, if the author is too oblivious, they will leave themselves open to getting scammed, sometimes with devastating consequences.

Your heirs are going to be busy being…your heirs. They have other things in their life that will interest them. Writing probably isn't their primary passion. They'll be just as prone to giving their power away as you are.

I would warn your heirs to be extra cautious of anyone who promises peace of mind by taking away key estate responsibilities in exchange for money. It doesn't mean these types of services are scams—they could very well be the opposite. But if your heirs are ever scammed, it will likely be through a service presenting itself in this manner.

Also consider making your heirs aware of The Alliance of Independent Authors, which does a very good job of exposing scammers. Writer Beware also does a great job of calling out unscrupulous service providers for the scam artists they are.

OTHER ESTATE ORGANIZATION ITEMS

Now that we have dodged the Silver Bullets of Doom, we can move into calmer territory.

The items discussed in this section won't sink your estate if you mess them up. I suppose you could if you screwed all of them up, but a single misstep here and there won't be the end of the world.

Any screw-ups moving forward will be a headache for your executor and your heirs. If you can plan around most or all of these headaches, you'll save your heirs a significant amount of unnecessary time, effort, and money.

PHYSICAL MAIL

If you have a business address, you need to consider what will happen to it after your death.

These days, authors get very little physical mail; almost everything is emailed or available digitally, but your situation may be different. For many, a business address is just a formality to shield their actual address from the public. After you die, any mail that goes to your business address will need to be stopped or forwarded to your executor.

A business address may be a physical, actual business address, but that is unlikely for most authors. Instead, your business address is probably a post office box or street address box. In my state, because I am not a sole proprietor, my state government doesn't permit me to use a post office box; I must use a real address instead. I have a box at my local United Parcel Service Store (UPS), which gives me an address that looks like a street address. These types of boxes probably exist in your country too.

A lesser-known and lesser-used option that some may use is a virtual mailing address. With a virtual mailing address, all mail goes to a physical address of a company that scans your mail so you can view it on a dashboard. Any items like checks or packages will be forwarded to your address. This way, you don't have to give your real address and you don't have to worry about having a physical box to check. These services are frequently used by expatriates.

In any case, you need to figure out how to stop unnecessary physical mail and forward important items such as bills or tax documents. Are there places that send you mail for your writing, such as publishers sending royalty statements, retailers sending tax documents, and so on?

ACTION ITEMS

- Record everywhere you receive physical mail for your executor.
- Write down any business mail you could potentially receive and determine where it needs to go after your death. Some suggestions to get you started include publisher royalty statements, annual tax documents, fan mail from readers (don't forget, your address is in the footer of your email newsletters!), legal letters, and so on.
- Opt-in for digital documents wherever it makes sense. I'm a millennial, so of course, I'm going to tell you to go digital wherever and whenever possible, but do what works best for you. If you are a paper person, then you need to be extremely organized and take steps to protect your valuable papers.

- When you have a final list of potential items that you could receive by mail, write those down for your executor along with the contact information for the senders so your executor knows how to change the mailing address on file. It's always better to start at the source if you want to stop mail.

- If your executor must go to the post office to settle your affairs, write down the address of your post office and the names of the forms they will need to ask for. It sounds silly to do this, but trust me that it will save your executor time, especially if they don't live in your area. If you elect paper mailings, let your executor know if a digital option exists for each particular mail item, as your executor may want digital copies instead.

- If you use a post office box or a street address box, write down the address and phone number of where the boxes are located. Read your box agreement to see what your executor needs to do upon your death. You may not want to close the box; you may want your executor to transfer the box to his or her name. Find out how the transfer process works and leave those instructions for your executor.

- It's probably wise to have your executor forward your mail for at least one year to eighteen months just in case any unexpected important mail arrives. If there is an expense associated with this, learn it now and build it into your anticipated estate expenses. (My Aussie friends, for example, can get twelve months of free mail redirection from the Australia Post. Americans, on the other hand, have to pay for everything.)

- If your heirs will continue email marketing in your estate's name, don't forget to have them change the physical address at the bottom of your email footers. (Why would they continue email marketing, you ask? What if your heirs release a new edition of one of your books or they sign a licensing deal for one of your books? Don't you

think your existing readers will want to
know about it?)

- Your heirs will also need to update your
  business address with your domain and
  website hosting provider, on both your
  account details and in the WHOIS
  database.

YOUR BUSINESS FILES

Your business files are the files needed to run your business. They include:

- Expenses
- Sales reports
- Tax returns
- Contracts with service providers, licensing contracts, and product keys
- Any other documents you use to make decisions about your writing business

EXPENSES

I imagine that you keep track of your expenses in some form, whether it be printing them out, saving them in the cloud, or using software like QuickBooks or Xero. Most people don't have any issues here. The key is to make sure your expenses are organized in a way that your heirs can understand.

Also, there is a benefit to your heirs knowing when you paid for something and how much you paid for it. Knowing that you paid $300 for a book edit would prevent them from paying $1000 if they ever wanted to hire an editor for a posthumous work of similar length, for example.

SALES AND INCOME

How will your heirs know how well each of your books is selling, and on what retailers?

If you don't track your sales everywhere, your heirs only have half of the financial picture. And if you give them a mountain of sales reports for every retailer to wade through, that's not productive either.

Think about it: if you publish wide to Amazon, Apple, Audible, Google Play, IngramSpark, Kobo, Draft2Digital, Smashwords, PublishDrive, and StreetLib, that's ten different vendors. If your publishing career spans at least 20 years and you receive sales reports monthly, that's at least 2,400 reports, if you were diligent enough to save them all. Oh my…

If possible, find a way to make reviewing your sales easy while you're alive. If you're interested, I wrote a book called **The Author Income Problem** that tackles the challenge of aggregating all your historical and future sales reports. It's not easy, but your heirs will be glad you did it.

If you make affiliate income or income from other miscellaneous sources, that needs to be tracked too.

. . .

TAX RETURNS

Many countries audit tax returns. As we discussed in the Taxes chapter, you can be audited even after death.

If your heirs can't find records of your expenses, income, and tax returns, that could create a headache for them. When the government audits your tax returns, it will be more difficult for your heirs to justify an expense. As a result, your estate could pay more in taxes, which is a shame if it could have been avoided legally.

CONTRACTS

If you sign a contract, you need to keep a copy of it. The most common contracts you may sign are contracts with service providers like editors or cover designers. Keep those on file indefinitely.

You may also sign licensing contracts to license your copyright to someone for money. Definitely keep a copy of those contracts in case there is a dispute.

I would also consider keeping copies of any product licenses you purchase, like those of your writing apps or other programs you use in your writing business.

Read the terms of your licenses to see if they can be transferred. If your heir needs to use them, they will likely have to install the program on their computers, and having the proper license without having to hunt for it makes everything easier.

SAFEGUARDING YOUR BUSINESS FILES

I strongly recommend that you follow the tips in the Your Book Files chapter about backing up your work. If you're a paper person, that's fine, but you should still keep digital copies of your records in the event of a disaster.

. . .

ACTION ITEMS

- Keep good records of your business files
  and tell your heirs where to find them. This
  includes expenses, sales reports, tax
  returns, and contracts.

SOCIAL MEDIA ACCOUNTS

Oh, social media.

When people think about a "digital afterlife," they think of social media.

Some social media companies address your death and give you tools to determine what you want to happen to your accounts after you die.

The key question in this chapter to discuss with your heirs is whether they intend to use social media to market your work. If so, they may be better off creating new accounts that make it clear that the profiles are your estate. Otherwise, if you have followers, they may be confused and not know you're dead. Some people might prefer that, but I think readers should be notified and know when they are engaging with the author or his or her estate. More on this later in the book.

Also, I wouldn't bet on any social media company providing login details if your heirs don't have them. Your heirs are SOL if you don't leave usernames and passwords.

Let's go through the major social media companies (at the time of this writing) and look at their policies. The social media landscape is always changing, so if you don't see your preferred service in this chapter, do your own research.

(This chapter assumes that you have a minimal social media presence. If you're an influencer, read the next chapter.)

FACEBOOK AND INSTAGRAM (META)

. . .

Facebook (and Instagram) offer the most robust options for heirs. Everything in this chapter applies to both services.

It's important to understand that Facebook's and Instagram's terms of service explicitly forbid anyone other than you to use your account. Don't violate their terms.

Instead, Facebook and Instagram both offer three choices that you can use to specify what happens to your account after your death:

- The companies can delete your account upon being notified of your death.
- You can memorialize your account, which will clearly communicate to your friends that you have passed away. You specify a memorial contact who can manage your account, accept friend requests on your behalf, and pin a tribute to your profile.
- You can delete your account before you pass away.

You should decide what happens to your account while you're alive. If you die without making a designation, your heirs' only choice will be to log in to your account to delete (which is a violation of Facebook's and Instagram's terms), or contact Facebook and Instagram, fill out paperwork, answer a lot of questions, and spend time that they otherwise wouldn't have had to spend if you were organized to begin with.

It only takes a few seconds to decide what happens to your accounts. I set my designations in less than five minutes.

The next question is whether you have Facebook pages connected to your account. They will be deleted or frozen, depending on what you decide.

The next question is what happens to your Facebook ads. I would recommend that you keep detailed records of your ads and how you run them if they will be an important part of your author platform after death. Your heirs will need to recreate ads using their Facebook account. The good thing about Facebook ads is that they can be recreated much more easily than Amazon Ads.

. . .

LINKEDIN

It is a violation of LinkedIn's terms to share your password with anyone. They do not offer any tools to help you decide what will happen with your account when you die.

Unless you use LinkedIn somehow to sustain your book sales, your heirs probably won't need it after you die. You could either delete your account before you die or instruct your heirs to log in and delete your account. It's technically a violation of terms, but if deleting the account is all your heirs will do, I don't see any harm in that until or unless LinkedIn offers a better solution.

There is a process for notifying LinkedIn of a death, but it requires your heirs to gather a lot of paperwork. If your heirs have your login credentials and can delete your account in just a couple of minutes...

. . .

PINTEREST, SNAPCHAT, TWITTER, TIKTOK, AND VIRTUALLY EVERY OTHER SOCIAL MEDIA SITE

Your heirs can log in to delete your account or email the companies' care teams to let them know you've died. The care teams will ask for a lot of paperwork.

In the future, I expect more social media companies to do what Facebook is doing, as it balances flexibility with practicality. The truth is that you can't tweet, pin, connect, or make TikTok videos from the afterlife, so your heirs are unlikely to need these accounts when running your author estate. If they do need to use social media, they should create new accounts in the name of your estate.

ACTION ITEMS

- Decide what you want your heirs to do with your social media accounts after you pass away. Review the options available at all of the websites where you have an account.

- Preserve your usernames, passwords, and two-factor authentication so that your heirs can act according to your final wishes.

INFLUENCER PLATFORMS

If you're an influencer and have a substantial social media following, or a popular blog, podcast, and/or YouTube channel, you have extra work to do.

First, when you die, your influencer brand freezes. Unless you have designated someone to succeed you, there won't be any more content. You are the brand. However, the existing content you do have is probably monetized, or if it's not, it may still be a discovery vehicle for future readers to find your work.

Let's go through a few of the major influencing types and discuss your options.

. . .

BLOG

If you have a popular blog, you may be making decent Google AdSense or Amazon Associates revenue. It might also feed into a big email list, merchandise, or paid courses.

A blog is also a source of opportunities. Your heirs may be contacted by someone who wants to do a licensing deal for your books because they read something on your blog.

I believe you have a few options:

- Delete the blog. This may be a good idea if your content will become outdated quickly.
- Repurpose the blog into other content that can be sold. Your heirs could turn the blog into a book, for example. Then, you could either keep the blog or delete it.
- Keep the blog and maintain it. Your heirs

would need to monitor the posts, traffic, and keep the content relevant. They could hire guest writers or continue in your spirit. They could also respond to comments on existing posts and use social media to continue driving traffic to popular posts.

- Keep the blog and memorialize it. Make it clear that you are deceased and that there will be no additional posts. The blog exists mainly as a monument to your legacy and to help or entertain anyone who stumbles upon it. At some point, your heirs could retire it.

- Sell it. If you put a value on the work, your heirs can sell the content. I don't recommend this, but it is an option. This happens more often in the world of blogging than you might think.

The older your blog is and the more traffic you receive, the more complicated your situation will be.

. . .

PODCASTS

When you create a podcast, you create an account with a hosting provider like Libsyn or Blubrry. There are free podcast hosting options, but most people use a paid service.

Your podcast will be available as long as you pay your bill. It's very much like your website.

A podcast can be an amazing source of income and opportunities, and if your show has built up a substantial following, it may be unwise to delete it. Most podcast hosting providers charge a monthly fee based on how many megabytes of audio you upload each month. When you pass away, your heirs can change your plan to the lowest tier (once they have legal permission to do so). You will need to budget for this in your estate plan. Once traffic dwindles to critically low levels, your heirs can retire the show.

While you're alive, consider capping the show with a final episode that explains that you are no longer doing episodes. Record it and keep it somewhere your heirs can access to upload it posthumously. This isn't required, but I think it looks professional and shows your audience that you thought about them.

YOUTUBE

YouTube channels can be a source of income for heirs, and that income can persist a long time into the future as long as the videos are available, discoverable, and monetized.

YouTube does not have an inactivity policy, but a channel could still be deleted if the attached Gmail account is inactive for longer than two years (and if there is no additional activity on the account). That would trigger the Google account to be deleted.

I stumbled upon a (rather morbid) Wiki that contained links to dozens of deceased YouTubers and their dates of death. I checked at least two dozen links, and without exception, all of the channels were still active, even channels whose creators passed away more than two years ago.

I observed a few different things:

- Some channels were completely inactive. One of them was inactive for 13 years.
- Some channels were still posting content. It appeared to be compilation content.
- Some channels posted weird videos that had nothing to do with the channel, usually of a very short nature.

From this research, I drew three theories:

- Google enforces its inactivity rule, but they may only be enforcing it in certain situations.
- YouTube may have a different (private) inactivity policy than the Google master account, if they have one. If a Google

account has a YouTube channel with a moderate level of activity (views, comments, and so on), Google may not take action.

- If Google does take action either based on its master terms, the creator's heirs are circumventing an inactivity shutdown by posting content occasionally, and/or they are logging in to the channel regularly so that they comply with the Google master policy terms of service.

If I were a YouTuber whose channel is monetized and makes substantial income, I would instruct my heirs to keep the account active by logging in and posting a compilation video every once in a while. That may be enough to keep the channel active, earning money, and generating potential opportunities.

When you upload videos to YouTube, you grant them "a worldwide, non-exclusive, royalty-free, sublicensable and transferable license to use [your content] (including to reproduce, distribute, prepare derivative works, display and perform it) in connection with the Service and YouTube's (and its successors' and Affiliates') business, including for the purpose of promoting and redistributing part or all of the Service."

Contrary to popular belief, you do not assign them your copyright, and the license is not perpetual or irrevocable. So YouTube is not under any obligation to keep your work available forever, but they don't appear to be in a big hurry to delete it.

OTHER INFLUENCER CONSIDERATIONS

As an influencer, you have an impact on people's lives. Your death will sadden them. You owe it to them to think about how you will communicate your death to them and allow them to grieve. If it suits your personality, consider writing a blog post, podcast episode, or video that your heirs can release posthumously.

. . .

ACTION ITEMS

- Develop a communication plan with your followers.
- Give your heirs options on what they can do with your platform when you're gone.

EMAIL MARKETING

Email marketing is an important part of author marketing.

You own your email list, so your heirs should know about it. They can use it to notify your subscribers of your death and posthumous releases.

You'll need to read your email marketing service's terms to see what happens upon the death of a customer. No matter what happens, a unique (and very good) thing about email marketing platforms is that you own your list. Your heirs can download a CSV of your subscribers' names and emails at any time.

If your heirs contact your subscribers, they should be careful to let them know that the email is from your estate and that they are being emailed because they originally opted-in to your email list when you were alive. Subscribers should always have the option of unsubscribing at any time, and I would imagine that many people will unsubscribe the moment they learn of your death. That's okay.

If your heirs will actively manage your estate, I would encourage them not to discard email marketing, as your email list contains your biggest fans.

ACTION ITEMS

- Decide if your heirs should use email marketing after your death. If so, exercise some forethought about how you'd like for them to do it.

MISCELLANEOUS INCOME STREAMS

You may also have miscellaneous income sources that need to be addressed after your death.

Because these income streams are rare for most authors, I won't be going into the ins and outs of each one. If you have an exposure, you probably already know it, and you should know what to do if you've read this far.

AFFILIATE MARKETING

. . .

If you do any kind of affiliate marketing, you will probably have many dashboards you must use to track your income.

If you're deep into affiliate marketing, you might have just as many dashboards as you do book retailers. Every affiliate platform is different. Companies can change affiliate platforms too, which makes things a little more complicated.

All of these income sources need to be tracked and accounted for. Your heirs will need to update the account name and banking information on file once they have legal permission to do so. Otherwise, they will miss out on income that doesn't require any work on their part.

Also, be aware of what I call "ghost affiliate income," which is income that comes out of nowhere. I have one product that I promote where the company doesn't have a dashboard. I have no way of knowing if I make referral sales. However, the company sends me a direct deposit every month with a thank you letter. It's always a surprise. I definitely want to let my heirs know to update my contact info on file with this company! But my heirs won't know that the income source even exists unless I tell them.

Affiliate income is ridiculously easy money that your heirs should continue receiving after you're gone.

COACHING AND CONSULTATIONS

Unless you've figured out how to coach people from the grave, your coaching services will end.

There are many ways to set up coaching packages. Some coaches charge after meeting with a client, but some charge upfront.

Many people also use automation so that they don't have to go back and forth with clients to find an appropriate time to meet.

If your calendar is available to book without you approving it first, your main preoccupation should be making sure that an unsuspecting customer doesn't sign up for a spot on your calendar after you're gone. If you have a platform set up for people to pay before a booking without clearing it first, then you especially want to avoid this because it would put your heirs in the unfortunate position of having to apologize and issue refunds.

There is also the possibility that you could die before a booked client meeting. Your heirs should have access to your calendar so they can proactively cancel any upcoming events. This also applies to any webinars or interviews you might have booked.

And if you die and don't let your heirs know about your coaching services and don't leave passwords so that your heirs don't even know this is happening…you're going to have some very, very angry customers who may retaliate with credit card chargebacks and threatening letters, which will cause a headache for your estate. Most people are understanding about this sort of thing, but they will want their money back.

Also, keep in mind and plan for the fact that if your coaching income is significant, your heirs will see a significant reduction in income.

CROWDFUNDING

If you engage in crowdfunding projects, make sure you have a contingency plan in place in case you pass away during a campaign. If you successfully fund a campaign, your heirs may be obligated to fulfill the promises you made, especially if there are contracts in place with manufacturers and suppliers to create physical products. Your heirs need to know about any contracts you sign.

The ins and outs of crowdfunding are also outside the scope of this book.

LICENSING DEALS

. . .

You may have signed miscellaneous licensing deals that need to be accounted for.

For example, I published an essay in a reputable magazine that promised to pay me if they reprinted the article in the future. They also compiled my article in a book, for which they owed me money per our contract.

I also have occasional royalties due to me from other contracts I've signed over the years. That's the beautiful nature of copyright.

Your heirs would need to know about deals like this so that they can collect the money and make future licensing deals!

PAID COURSES

If you offer paid courses through a platform like Teachable or Kajabi, then you should review the company's terms and contact them to see what happens after you die and how your heirs can continue enjoying the income from your courses.

If you offer tech support or customer service as part of a course, or if you hire assistants to help you in the everyday nuts and bolts of the course, you have another exposure that we'll discuss in the outsourcing chapters.

In any case, make sure you have backups of your course materials in case your heirs will need them.

PATREON

If you have a Patreon account, it should be discontinued unless your heirs can continue offering the promised benefits, which is unlikely. Your social media and influencer communication plan should include your patrons.

Closing your Patreon account will constitute cutting off an income source, so plan accordingly.

ACTION ITEMS

- If you have miscellaneous income sources, such as affiliate dashboards, coaching, crowdfunding, miscellaneous licensing deals, paid courses, and Patreon, inventory them and come up with a plan for each one.

TRADITIONALLY-PUBLISHED WORKS

If you have traditionally-published books either through a large publisher or a small press, then you have some work to do.

First, you need to store copies of all publishing contracts, correspondence, and royalty statements for your heirs.

Second, you need to reread your contracts and decide if you want your heirs to keep receiving the royalties or if you eventually want them to get the rights back…if they can.

Third, once it is safe to do so, your heirs need to contact the publisher, provide proof of your death, and advise them where to send the royalty statements. It may not be this simple.

Your heirs should also beware of literary agents and, if the royalty payments are coming from the agent directly, they should scrutinize all statements. If you're dealing with an unscrupulous actor, there could be embezzlement if your heirs don't pay attention. (There could be embezzlement while you're alive too, but we won't go there.)

Whatever your situation is, you're governed by the contract you signed. Hopefully, you understood what you signed. Otherwise, it may be up to your heirs to clean up the mess.

There are many resources for traditionally-published authors, and you should make sure that your traditionally-published contracts are included in your estate planning.

ACTION ITEMS

- Make sure your heirs understand the nature

of any traditionally-published contracts that you have signed.

- Instruct your heirs where your contracts are located and how to update the address and bank account on file so they can continue to receive the royalty checks.
- If you signed a bad contract, explain it to your heirs and how they might go about reverting the rights if you are unable to do it in your lifetime.

COAUTHORS AND COLLABORATIONS

Writing books with another person is a popular way to co-market and grow your writing platform.

However, coauthoring presents some unique problems with estate management.

No one should enter a coauthor agreement without a written contract. Both authors need to be on the same page.

In most coauthor situations, both authors own the copyright equally. But does your coauthor agreement indicate what happens when one of you dies?

Both authors could decide that the copyright transfers to the other person upon one author's death. Then, when the final author dies, the rights transfer to that person's heirs. In my opinion, this is a raw deal, but there may be a good reason to do it, especially if one of the authors doesn't have any heirs to pass the work down to.

Or, the authors could decide that if one author dies, the surviving author will continue paying royalties to the deceased author's heirs. This is how I imagine most authors prefer to operate, and I will assume this arrangement for the rest of the chapter.

The first most obvious question is how your surviving coauthor will know that you have died. Do you talk regularly? If not, they may not know of your passing. You will need to keep their contact information up-to-date so that your heirs can notify them. This includes the contact information of your heirs. You'll need your coauthor's heir information too.

There are many Pandora's boxes here that may require the advice of a lawyer. What if both authors live in different countries? What if one author gets divorced? Does the ex-spouse have a claim to royalties? Coauthoring can get complicated.

The next thing you should determine is who publishes the book. In a coauthor arrangement, one of the authors must act as the publisher. This author is responsible for uploading the book, maintaining it, and paying royalties to the coauthor.

If you're the publisher, then this will be a burden for your heirs. Assuming your heirs don't want this responsibility (because why would they?), you should discuss with your coauthor what will happen if you pass. It may be wise for your heirs to pull the book down and for your coauthor to republish it and pay them royalties. Of course, I'm presuming that you picked a reputable and trustworthy coauthor.

If you're the publisher and your heirs don't know that, you could expose them to headaches, copyright infringement allegations, and lawsuits. After all, you are contractually obligated to pay your coauthor. You'd be upset if you didn't get paid too!

If you're not the publisher, then your heirs can update the banking information with the publishing author so that the money gets deposited into the right account.

Coauthoring is great for business, but the royalty side is a real pain. Consider using a service like Draft2Digital's Paid Collaborator tool. With this tool, the publisher author uploads the book to Draft2Digital and adds the coauthor as a paid collaborator. Draft2Digital then splits the royalties.

If you can split your royalties with minimal hassle when you're alive, then arranging the payments after your death will just be a formality for your heirs. This also allows both authors to honor their original commitment and support the other's heirs in the event of an untimely death.

ACTION ITEMS

- Store your coauthor agreement in a safe place. If it doesn't mention what happens when one of the coauthors dies, amend it immediately.

- Keep your coauthor's contact info up-to-date. Make sure they have your most current contact information too. This should also include the contact information for each coauthor's next of kin.
- If you are the publisher, discuss this responsibility with your heirs and your coauthor and determine if you want your heirs to continue as the publisher or if it would be better for the coauthor to reupload the book and pay your heirs.
- If you are not the publisher, make sure the heirs provide the correct contact information to the surviving coauthor.
- Consider using Draft2Digital's Paid Collaborator tool to simplify the administration of royalties while you're alive.

YOUR HEIRS' OPERATING SYSTEMS

What operating system does your heir use? It sounds like a silly question, but it could create a headache.

I'm an Apple guy. I always have been and I always will be. I also happen to have Windows and Linux installed on my machine just in case I need them. But for most of my needs, I always use MacOS first.

My wife hates Apple products. Any time she has to use my computer, she walks away frustrated.

If she has to manage my estate by using my Mac computer, I probably won't have an estate!

Therefore, it is incumbent upon me to figure out how my wife can run my estate by migrating everything over to a Windows computer. That's not as difficult as it seems. It just requires some forethought about the apps and services I use.

I highly suggest you think about this in your estate planning. For example, if you use a Mac-only writing app and don't have your manuscripts backed up in an alternate format such as Microsoft Word docs or rich text files, your heirs won't be able to open your manuscripts on their computers. They'll have to follow a few steps to access your work.

Will this sink your estate? Probably not, but it will create friction.

ACTION ITEMS

- If your heir prefers a different operating system than the one you use to run your writing business, be thoughtful about how they can transition your work to their computer.

BOOKMARKS

In your primary web browser, you **do** have bookmarks with all the sites you use regularly, right?

Otherwise, how will your heirs know where to log in to all of your accounts? At many places, they can figure out where they need to go with ease—at others, not so much.

My bookmarks used to be a mess until I cleaned them up.

I recommend that you organize your bookmarks logically so that your heir knows what they are and can navigate through them easily. Try to keep it simple and be thoughtful about how you name your bookmarks too. If there are any sites you visit frequently that aren't bookmarked, rectify that now.

Your heir may use a different browser than you, and if they're not tech-savvy, you may need to leave instructions on how to export bookmarks from one browser to another. Fortunately, this is not hard and only takes a couple of minutes.

ACTION ITEMS

- Organize your web browser bookmarks thoughtfully while you are alive. Note which browser you use so your heirs can export your bookmarks easily.

FREELANCERS AND VIRTUAL ASSISTANTS

Outsourcing means hiring someone else to perform a task that you can't or don't want to do yourself. Most people think of outsourcing as hiring a virtual assistant, but hiring an editor or cover designer is also a form of outsourcing.

If you outsource any part of your business, there are a few things you should consider.

CURRENT PROJECTS

. . .

On January 1, you hire a cover designer. The designer promises to send you a draft by January 15. You pass away on January 14.

Your designer will need feedback on your cover, but they will also need to be paid.

As long as your heirs have access to your email, they should be able to discover the problem. But it might be a few days or weeks until they check your email unless you tell them that your emails need to be checked daily for any outstanding projects.

(Just remember, your heirs can't spend your money without talking to a lawyer.)

Another variation on this problem is for services that you pay escrow. On freelancing platforms, you pay the fee upfront, and when the work is completed to your satisfaction, you release it. Generally (but not always), your credit card is charged the full amount when you make the purchase, so the payment isn't an issue, but your heirs will still have to release the payment to the freelancer. Otherwise, the freelancer could file a dispute, which will cause a headache.

Also, this advice doesn't apply just to your death. It applies if you are incapacitated too. Your disablement doesn't mean you can escape previous contractual obligations.

VIRTUAL ASSISTANTS

Virtual assistants pose additional problems.

If you hire a VA, it is usually to do ongoing tasks that you need help with. You must provide instructions to your VA, oversee their work and provide feedback as necessary, and then pay them.

If you die, your VA:

- Might be in the middle of a job.
- Might not immediately know that you passed away and may therefore keep working, accruing additional expense.
- Will suddenly be fired.

Make plans to address this and make sure your VA(s) are included on a list of immediate people to contact after your death. VAs are people too, and they may grieve your death. More importantly, they will need to find another job because they were depending on your income.

You should also consider summarizing what the VA(s) does for you. Your heir might want to keep contracting with them!

PART-TIME AND FULL-TIME EMPLOYEES

If you hire employees of any kind, you're playing by a different set of rules and need to include them in your estate planning.

ACTION ITEMS

- Determine how heirs will find out about in-flight projects after your death.

- Include regular freelancers in your heir's death notifications.

COPYRIGHT LICENSING RISKS

Most authors hire cover designers. However, most authors and designers usually do not execute signed contracts.

This means that, by default, a designer owns the copyright to the cover and they license it to the author. This also means that the designer can revoke the author's license at any time.

Unless you signed a contract that says you own the copyright, the cover artist can revoke their license at any time for any reason.

It's unlikely that a designer would revoke their license, but it could happen. If a designer doesn't like your politics, or if you are accused of sexual harassment, they would be within their rights to disassociate from you or your estate. This would create a headache for your heirs because they would have to scramble to replace your cover everywhere it is present.

In the United States, if you signed a contract that says that you own the copyright, the designer can still come back and revert the rights under the principle of copyright termination. There are specific ways to avoid this risk, but they require the help of a lawyer to help you draft appropriate contract language. A designer may not be willing to agree to such language, or they may negotiate a higher fee for it. But you may want to think about reducing this potential risk while you're alive.

If you're not in the US and are thinking this doesn't apply to you, think again. In many countries around the world, artists also have moral rights, one of which is the right to be associated with a work. Even if a designer licenses a design for the life of a copyright, they may still retain (and assert) moral rights, which could cause headaches for your heirs.

Moral rights are outside the scope of this book. If you're not familiar with them, I recommend that you educate yourself on the concept. I've included some helpful copyright resources in the Appendix.

Don't let a rights revocation come out of left field for your heirs. It's always a smart idea to document all content and media that you license for use in your business in the unlikely event of a revocation.

ACTION ITEMS

- Document all licenses to all content and media you use in your business. Note any reversion or termination risks and draft a contingency plan.

POSTHUMOUS WORK

What to do with posthumous work is a decision every author must make.

Do you want your heirs to release posthumous work? Do you want to forbid posthumous work? Whatever you decide, you should discuss it with your attorney when you draft your last will.

Posthumous work is deeply divisive. If a work is labeled posthumous, readers will automatically have a bias against it. But, it could drive income to the estate (even if it is ultimately at the expense of its reputation.)

. . .

FUTURE EDITIONS AND EDITS

Is it okay for your heirs to reedit your books or issue new editions? In the right hands, your heirs will treat your works with care. In the wrong hands, they will bastardize it. In the case of the latter, that will put readers off.

YOUR CURRENT WORK-IN-PROGRESS

There's another posthumous work you should consider: your current work-in-progress when you pass away. Unless you die immediately after publishing your work, chances are high that you'll be working on at least one project at the time of an unexpected death.

Do you want your heirs to hire someone to finish it, as Robert Jordan's estate did with the **Wheel of Time** series? Do you want the work released as-is so readers can draw their conclusions about what could have happened? Do you want the work burned so that readers will never see it? Discuss this with your heirs.

My opinion is that if your WIP is mostly complete, tell your heirs to get it done. If you outlined the book, then a ghostwriter can pick up where you left off. Even if you didn't outline, a good ghostwriter can fill in the gaps. It's easy money for your estate. But that's just me.

ACTION ITEMS

- Decide how you want posthumous work to be handled. This includes unfinished work and any works-in-progress at the time of your death.

TAKING CARE OF YOUR READERS

Don't forget about your readers. When they read your books, they develop a relationship with you. Honor them in your passing too.

CURRENT AND PAST READERS

Your current readers will likely mourn your death. Consider providing a space for them to pay their respects, grieve, and celebrate your life.

Also, consider some bonuses for them as a thank you for their support. This could include a posthumous short story or novel that you wrote intending to release upon your death, a heartfelt thank you video, or something else creative.

I've always thought it would be cool to write one novel per year that I don't publish; instead, my estate would release it posthumously. This way, current readers continue getting books from me beyond the grave for a certain period after my death. I write anywhere from 10-15 books per year, so I can afford to do this.

Readers who enjoyed your books in the past but who may have forgotten about you will be saddened to hear about your death. They may want to pick up more of your books out of respect or renewed interest. This is why it is critical to keep all your books available for sale so that readers can buy your books.

FUTURE READERS

New readers will continue to discover your books. You should include them in your estate plans too.

If your author brand sees heightened success and recognition after your death, readers will be curious about you. Look at the most common FAQs for mega-bestselling authors and answer those questions in a book or video series. Answer as many questions as you can. Release them while you're alive or posthumously. This also would give your estate an out for common emails that readers may send via your contact form.

Give future readers a way to pay their respects too. You never know how one of your books can impact someone's life. I think it would bring comfort to your heirs to know what an impact your legacy is having; it will keep your heirs motivated too.

ACTION ITEMS

- Determine how you want your readers to be notified of your death.
- Determine how to give them a space to grieve.
- Consider releasing posthumous bonuses for them as a thank you.
- Consider how future readers will find your work and their needs.

PREPARING EVERYTHING FOR YOUR HEIRS

Now it's time for the time-consuming (and possibly painful) process of putting everything together into an author estate plan. You understand the different parts of your author ecosystem now and how everything fits together.

Help your heirs A.I.M. for the stars by considering how they will access, understand, and manage the different parts of your author ecosystem.

But I suspect that this book has probably been a little overwhelming for you and you've been thinking, "How do I organize it all?"

First, keep it as simple as possible. Remember, your heirs need simplicity. Organize all your materials as if your heir has no clue what you're talking about.

When you're gone, your heirs will have a lot to handle before they even get to your author estate. Make it easy on them.

I also believe your heirs should have one place where they can go to find answers to everything. As authors, we need to resist the urge to overcomplicate things.

I CREATED AN ORGANIZER FOR YOU

If the thought of putting everything together still overwhelms you and your heirs are open to digital files, I've put together a free, friendly Microsoft Excel template that will save you time and break this into easy steps for you. All you have to do is fill in the blanks and modify as you need. You can store the organizer digitally, and your heirs can also print it out if they prefer. You can grab it at www. authorlevelup.com/estateplanorganizer.

The Estate Plan Organizer is not a legal document. It is merely a tool to help you wrangle all the different aspects of your business together. Your executor will appreciate the work, and your attorney will appreciate it too!

I've also included an Appendix in this book that summarizes all the action items so you can get through them quickly. Do it at your own pace. Remember, this is a lot of stuff, and it doesn't have to be done overnight. Knock off an item or two per week until you're done. Then, review your estate plan once a year.

(If you use the Estate Plan Organizer, it mirrors the book and the action items I listed.)

WRITING A FINAL LETTER TO YOUR HEIRS

. . .

When you're done, sit down with your heirs and go through it with them a few pages at a time. Get them as comfortable as you can. They'll never be 100 percent ready, but trust me, if you follow the advice in this book, they'll be in a far better position than most.

Once your heirs understand the estate plan and you've made appropriate modifications, consider following up with a final letter that you can include along with the plan.

I recommend M.L. Buchman's excellent book **Estate Planning for Authors: Your Final Letter (and why you should write it now!)**. Not only is it a fantastic estate planning book, M.L. includes a template you can use that explains the publishing business in plain English to your heirs. I adopted his letter and am using it in my estate plan.

An important warning about your final letter is to be careful not to make anything prescriptive. You don't want it to clash with your will. Anything and everything in it should be a suggestion at best. Otherwise, it could cause legal trouble.

Also, I would recommend supplementing the letter with short instructional videos where needed. For example, if you use an app that is not immediately intuitive, make a quick video showing your heirs how to use it and some common things they may need it for.

YOU CAN DO THIS

I don't think anyone realizes just how complicated author estate planning is when they decide to write their first book. If they did, we'd have a lot fewer authors!

But just as you learned how to write that first book, you too can organize your estate and create a lasting legacy. With the help of a skilled financial adviser, accountant, estate attorney, and intellectual property attorney, you and your heirs will be dangerous.

Is it easy? No, but we don't choose to do anything in life because it's easy. We do it because we love it.

And I know that after reading this book, you'll be able to do it.

I've taught you everything I know about estate planning, so start planning your estate today!

GET MY ESTATE PLAN ORGANIZER

If you have been thinking "how am I going to organize all this stuff" as you read this book, let me save you some time and energy.

I've put together an easy-to-use Estate Plan Organizer in Microsoft Excel that will help you get organized quickly. The organizer includes all action items from this book. You just have to fill in the blanks.

Feel free to add to it and modify it to your heart's content. You can even add your personal estate information to it so that all your estate plan information is in one place.

The organizer is also printer-friendly in case your heirs are paper people.

Get instant access today at www.authorlevelup. com/estateplanorganizer. No email address required. Download and enjoy!

READ NEXT: THE AUTHOR HEIR HANDBOOK

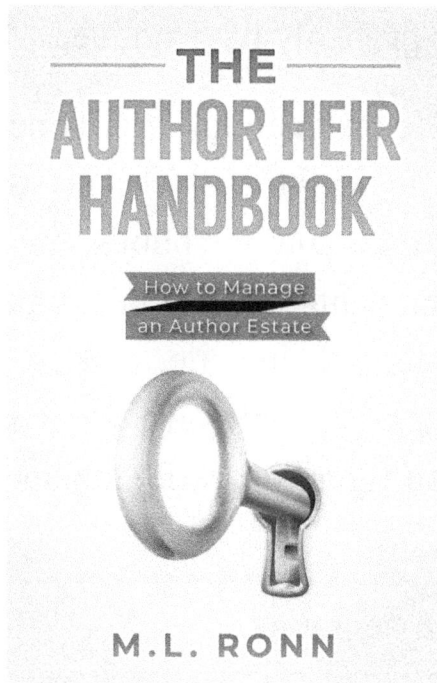

THE
AUTHOR HEIR HANDBOOK

How to Manage
an Author Estate

M.L. RONN

(The perfect book for the person inheriting your estate!)

An author has died. You're responsible for managing their estate, and it's a mess.

Are you overwhelmed? Frustrated?

You might be feeling that this responsibility the author gave you is more of a burden than a gift.

You know that managing the author's books will make money and provide for you and the author's heirs, but you probably have no idea where to start.

The Author Heir Handbook is a concise guide for heirs written in PLAIN ENGLISH that will help you understand an author's publishing business, the different components that the deceased author used to create books and income, and how to manage those components. It will save you countless hours by helping you figure out where to spend your time and effort.

This book will help you:

* Avoid making mistakes that could cripple the estate

* Locate the author's manuscripts

* Take an inventory of all the author's works (with an easy template to save time)

* Determine which online accounts the author used (and how to access them)

* Manage the money

* Get hired help when you need it (and how to avoid scams)

* Keep the author's books relevant for new generations

* Create income for you and your family, the way the author intended

Managing an author estate is hard work, but this book will help simplify the process. You just might even be able to do more with the estate than the author ever could in their lifetime. Purchase your copy today, and don't do things the hard way!

Grab your copy of The Author Heir Handbook today at www.authorlevelup.com/heirhandbook.

MORE BOOKS BY M.L. RONN

Nonfiction/Books for Writers:

www.authorlevelup.com/books

Fiction:

www.michaellaronn.com/books

MEET M.L. RONN

Science fiction and fantasy on the wild side!

M.L. Ronn (Michael La Ronn) is the author of many science fiction and fantasy novels including **The Good Necromancer**, **Android X**, and **The Last Dragon Lord** series.

In 2012, a life-threatening illness made him realize that storytelling was his #1 passion. He's devoted his life to writing ever since, making up whatever story makes him fall out of his chair laughing the hardest. Every day.

Learn more about Michael
www.authorlevelup.com (for writers)
www.michaellaronn.com (fiction)

APPENDIX A: ACTION ITEMS

PLANNING YOUR ESTATE

Your Last Will and Testament

- Determine your last wishes and discuss them with all parties who will be in your will. Don't surprise anyone. The person you want to be your executor may not want the job. Make sure everyone agrees to serve your estate before moving forward.

- If you have a will, reread it. If it doesn't address your copyrights, rectify it ASAP.
- Whether you have a will or not, read a few books on wills and trusts so you understand the topic on more than a superficial level. Even the best attorneys in the world won't be able to help you if you can't communicate your desires.
- Find a licensed estate attorney who specializes in wills and trusts in your area (hint: use Google). Many people are intimidated by attorneys, but there's nothing to be afraid of. Find out if the attorney offers free consultations. If not, understand the attorney's price structures upfront so there are no surprises.
- Tell the attorney about your copyrights!
- Consider discussing a digital assets provisions in your will.
- Consult with a licensed copyright attorney in your area to double-check the estate attorney's work as it pertains to your copyrights. Or, choose a law firm that has both estate law and intellectual property as

practice areas. This way, your estate attorney can seek counsel in-house.

- Update your will after major life events, such as moving states, marriage, divorce, spousal death, the birth, coming of age, marriage, or death of a child, the death or incapacitation of anyone listed in your will as a beneficiary, and other events that could impact how your personal and literary estate will pass to your heirs.
- Your attorney will give you several copies of your will. Separate them and keep them in a safe place that you and your heirs will remember. Destroy all copies of old wills.

Your Living Will and Power(s) of Attorney

- Determine what you want to happen to you in the event you become incapacitated.
- Decide on who will have your medical power of attorney.
- Decide on other types of power of attorney

that are needed (financial, literary, digital, and so on).

Trusts

- Ask both your estate and copyright attorney if a trust is right for you, your family, and your copyrights.
- Ask the attorneys how copyright should be transferred to a will and when.

Other Fundamentals

- Buy life insurance.
- Invest in a fire-resistant safe and fire-resistant document bags for your estate planning documents.
- If you rent a safe deposit box, make sure your heirs know it exists, where the keys

are, and where they can find a copy of the box rental agreement.

- Decide on how you want your heirs to conduct your funeral and how you want your remains to be handled.
- Document the contact information of your service providers that your executor will need to contact after your death, such as your funeral home, estate lawyer, copyright lawyer, financial adviser, accountant, and life insurance company, to name a few.

Cataloging Your Property

- Create an inventory of all your intellectual property and keep it up-to-date.
- Create an inventory of all physical property owned by your publishing business.

ORGANIZING YOUR ESTATE

THE SILVER BULLETS OF DOOM

Passwords and Passcodes to Your Devices

- Write down your passwords and passcodes for your devices and tell your heirs where to find them.

Usernames and Passwords to Your Online Accounts

- Use a password manager to gather and store your passwords in a safe place.
- Secure the password manager with two-factor authentication using an authenticator app and a physical security key.
- Store your master password in a safe place.
- Use the password manager's emergency access feature to grant immediate access to

an heir upon your death. This is extra insurance in case they cannot find your master password.

Two-Factor Authentication (2FA)

- If you use a phone passcode, write it down or store it somewhere safe. Make sure you update the record whenever you change it.
- Enable 2FA wherever you can to protect your accounts.
- Document which sites you use 2FA on, and the method you use to get your passcode. (Download a spreadsheet template at www. authorlevelup.com/2fatemplate.)
- Leave clear instructions to your heirs where they can get your backup passcodes after you die.

Emails

- Read the terms of service for all email providers you use, and take care not to breach any terms when planning your estate.
- Inventory your email addresses for your executor along with usernames and passwords. Record what each email address is used for, how frequently you check it, and how you access it (i.e., by logging in to each account individually or using an email client on your desktop or phone).
- Inventory which of your online accounts use that email address. Your heirs will need to change the email address on file at all your online accounts after your death. (Hint: use a password manager to skip this step.)
- Read your email provider's terms of service. If you use Google, visit their Inactive Manager and designate a beneficiary for your data once your account is deleted after your death.
- Delete any email accounts you do not

need.

- Unsubscribe from as many email lists as you can and find ways to reduce your email volume.
- Consider combining your email inboxes with an email client and/or setting up forwarders for secondary email addresses so that your heirs will be able to access all future emails in one place.
- Consider setting up an autoresponder "from the grave" for future readers who fill out the contact form on your website.

Bank Accounts

- Make an inventory of all bank accounts you own personally and in your business. Include the names on the account, account, routing, debit and credit cards, PINs, bank deposit boxes, whether you have designated POD, and anything else that will help your executor get a clear financial picture of your estate.

- Make an inventory of all the income streams you have had, currently have, and anticipate having, and which bank account(s) each income stream flows into.
- Make an inventory of all the recurring expenses that are charged to your bank account, credit, or debit cards. Note whether each can be kept or canceled after your death.
- Find out how your bank(s) handles the death of a customer and note any differences for your executor.
- Discuss with your estate attorney the best way to avoid an asset freeze to keep your current bank assets available to your heirs.
- Discuss with your estate attorney the safest legal way to reroute the flow of future money; discuss when it can start and how to do it without making mistakes. Instructions will need to be communicated very clearly to your heirs.

- Discuss the tax ramifications of your strategy with your accountant.

Taxes

- Determine the potential value of your estate with and without your copyrights.
- Determine which estate and inheritance taxes apply to you and your heirs.
- Get your tax paperwork in order. Make plans to pay back taxes if you owe them. Don't die with a tax mess for your executor to clean up.
- Meet with your estate planning attorney and your accountant to plan your estate. Plan early, often, and regularly.

Book Files

- Make sure you are backing up your book

files religiously, automatically, and diligently.

- Practice the art of separation, diversification, and duplication regularly.
- Inform your heirs where your book files are located and how to access the backups if something were to happen.

Domain and Website

- Communicate the importance of maintaining your website to your heirs.
- Inventory all domains you have.
- Research your hosting provider's terms for changing the ownership on your account.
- If there is paperwork required, include a link to the form. Revisit the link every few years to make sure it's still valid. Save your heirs from having to dig around like I did.

Your Accounts at Book Retailers

- Preserve your account usernames, passwords, and two-factor authentication for your heirs.
- Review book retailers' terms of service and website details very carefully, and if necessary, contact their customer support team to learn how they treat deceased authors' accounts and what steps your heirs will need to take to secure your books.
- Inform your heirs that they must speak with a lawyer before taking any action on any accounts to avoid issues with probate.
- Have a conversation with your heirs about just how many accounts they will need to manage and if they are comfortable with that. While you're alive, work together to develop a plan that will make account management less burdensome for them when you're gone.

Other Estate Planning Items

Physical Mail

- Determine what your executor will do with your personal residential mail.
- Determine what your executor will do with any post office or street address mailboxes, and how to forward or stop any mail you are currently receiving.

Social Media

- Decide what you want your heirs to do with your social media accounts after you pass away. Review the options available at all of the websites where you have an account.
- Preserve your usernames, passwords, and two-factor authentication so that your heirs can act according to your final wishes.

Influencer Platforms

- Develop a communication plan with your followers.
- Give your heirs options on what they can do with your platform when you're gone.

Email Marketing

- Decide if your heirs should use email marketing after your death. If so, exercise some forethought about how you'd like for them to do it.

Business Files

- Keep good records of your business files and tell your heirs where to find them. This includes expenses, sales reports, tax returns, and contracts.

Miscellaneous Income Sources

- If you have miscellaneous income sources, such as affiliate dashboards, coaching, crowdfunding, paid courses, and Patreon, inventory them and come up with a plan for each one.

Traditionally-Published Books

- Make sure your heirs understand the nature of any traditionally-published contracts that you have signed.
- Instruct your heirs where your contracts are located and how to update the address and bank account on file so they can continue to receive the royalty checks.

- If you signed a bad contract, explain it to your heirs and how they might go about reverting the rights if you are unable to do it in your lifetime.

Coauthor and Collaborator Agreements

- Store your coauthor agreement in a safe place. If it doesn't mention what happens when one of the coauthors dies, amend it immediately.
- Keep your coauthor's contact info up-to-date. Make sure they have your most current contact information too. This should also include the contact information for each coauthor's next of kin.
- If you are the publisher, discuss this responsibility with your heirs and your coauthor and determine if you want your heirs to continue as the publisher or if it would be better for the coauthor to reupload the book and pay your heirs.

- If you are not the publisher, make sure the heirs provide the correct contact information to the surviving coauthor.
- Consider using Draft2Digital's Paid Collaborator tool to simplify the administration of royalties while you're alive.

Your Heir's Operating System

- If your heir prefers a different operating system to the one you use to run your writing business, be thoughtful about how they can transition your work to their computer.

Bookmarks

- Organize your web browser bookmarks thoughtfully while you are alive. Note which browser you use so your heirs can export your bookmarks easily.

Outsourcing

- Determine how heirs will find out about in-flight projects after your death.
- Include regular freelancers in your heir's death notifications.

Copyright Licensing Risks

- Document all licenses to all content and media you use in your business. Note any reversion or termination risks and draft a contingency plan.

Posthumous Work

- Decide how you want posthumous work to be handled. This includes unfinished work and any works-in-progress at the time of your death.

Your Readers

- Determine how you want your readers to be notified of your death.
- Determine how to give them a space to grieve.
- Consider releasing posthumous bonuses for them as a thank you.
- Consider how future readers will find your work and their needs.

APPENDIX B: HELPFUL RESOURCES
COPYRIGHT

If you need some primers on copyright and what you and your heirs can do with your work, check out the following resources.

The Copyright Handbook by Stephen Fishman.

"Harvard Law School's CopyrightX" series on YouTube: https://www. authorlevelup.com/Harvardcopyright

ESTATE PLANNING

. . .

Estate Planning for Authors: Your final letter (and why you should do it now!) by M.L Buchman

Estate Planning (in Plain English) by Leonard D. DuBoff and Amanda Bryan

Plan Your Estate by Denis Clifford

MORE BY M.L. RONN ON THIS TOPIC

Keep Your Books Selling

The Author Heir Handbook